The Progressive Era
and the Great War
1896–1920

GOLDENTREE BIBLIOGRAPHIES
In American History
under the series editorship of
Arthur S. Link

The Progressive Era and the Great War 1896–1920

SECOND EDITION

compiled by

William M. Leary, Jr.

University of Georgia

and

Arthur S. Link

Princeton University

AHM Publishing Corporation
Arlington Heights, Illinois 60004

ISBN: 0-88295-575-6, paper
ISBN: 0-88295-574-8, cloth

Library of Congress Card Number:
78-70030

PRINTED IN THE UNITED STATES OF AMERICA
788

Contents

Editor's Foreword   vii

Preface to the Second Edition   ix

Abbreviations   xi

I.   Bibliographical Guides and Selected Reference Works . .   1

II. American Politics from Theodore Roosevelt to Woodrow
            Wilson   2
     1. General   2
     2. Biographies, Autobiographies, and Collected
          Works   4
     3. The Progressive Movement   10
        A. General   10
        B. Progressivism in the Cities and States   12
        C. The Social Justice Movement   16
        D. The Social Gospel Movement   18
        E. The Muckrakers   19
        F. The Conservation Movement   19
        G. Agrarian Movements   20
        H. Intellectual Progressivism   21
     4. The Republican Era, 1901–1913   22
     5. The Wilson Era, 1913–1920   25
        A. General   25
        B. The New Freedom   27
        C. The First World War and After   29
     6. The Supreme Court   34
     7. Socialism   35

III. The United States and Its World Relations   36
     1. General   36
     2. Imperialism and the War with Spain   39
     3. The United States and Latin America   42
     4. The United States and Europe   44
     5. The United States and Asia   46

CONTENTS

6. The Road to War, 1914–1917   49
7. The First World War, Versailles, and the Great
         Betrayal   52

IV. The American People and Their Economic Institutions .   58
1. General   58
2. Demographic Changes   59
3. Concentration, Competition, and Public Policy   60
4. Finance Capitalism   61
5. Manufacturing and Other Industries   62
6. Transportation   65
7. Agriculture   66
8. Research and Technology   67
9. Labor   68
10. Immigrants and Immigration   73

V. Social and Intellectual Main Currents in American Life .   75
1. Social Trends and Changes   75
2. Currents of American Thought   77
3. Education   78
4. Science, Medicine, and Public Health   80
5. Religion   81
6. The Arts   83
7. Journalism   84
8. The Negro   85
9. Nativism   89
10. Women   91

Index   93
Notes   107

Editor's Foreword

Goldentree Bibliographies in American History are designed to provide students, teachers, and librarians with ready and reliable guides to the literature of American history in all its remarkable scope and variety. Volumes in the series cover comprehensively the major periods in American history, while additional volumes are devoted to all important subjects.

Goldentree Bibliographies attempt to steer a middle course between the brief list of references provided in the average textbook and the long bibliography in which significant items are often lost in the sheer number of titles listed. Each bibliography is, therefore, selective, with the sole criterion for choice being the significance—and not the age—of any particular work. The result is bibliographies of all works, including journal articles and doctoral dissertations, that are still useful, without bias in favor of any particular historiographical school.

Each compiler is a scholar long associated, both in research and teaching, with the period or subject of his volume. All compilers have not only striven to accomplish the objective of this series but have also cheerfully adhered to a general style and format. However, each compiler has been free to define his field, make his own selections, and work out internal organization as the unique demands of his period or subject have seemed to dictate.

The single great objective of *Goldentree Bibliographies in American History* will have been achieved if these volumes help researchers and students to find their way to the significant literature of American history.

Arthur S. Link

Preface to the Second Edition

The Progressive era continues to be a fruitful field for historical research. Indeed, the scholarship of recent years has made necessary a revision of this bibliography less than a decade after its first publication. We have sought to include most significant books and articles on American political history, and also to list the more important works in other fields to which special bibliographies in the series are devoted. In addition, we have cited selected doctoral dissertations, publications in foreign languages, memoirs, and collections of printed documents and other papers of special note. As we no doubt have overlooked items that merit inclusion, we would welcome suggestions from users of this work in order that future editions might be more complete.

We hope that the topical organization of this volume, combined with frequent cross-references, will facilitate its use.

Again, we trust that students will learn as much from using this bibliography as we learned in compiling it.

W.M.L., Jr.
A.S.L.

Abbreviations

Ag Hist	Agricultural History
Am Econ Rev	American Economic Review
Am Hist Rev	American Historical Review
Am J Int Law	American Journal of International Law
Am Pol Sci Rev	American Political Science Review
Am Q	American Quarterly
Am Sch	American Scholar
Ann Am Acad Pol Soc Sci	Annals, American Academy of Political and Social Science
Ann Assn Am Geog	Annals, Association of American Geographers
Bus Hist Rev	Business History Review
Cath Hist Rev	Catholic Historical Review
Church Hist	Church History
For Aff	Foreign Affairs
His-Am Hist Rev	Hispanic-American Historical Review
Int Lab Rev	International Labour Review
J Am Hist	Journal of American History
J Am Stat Assn	Journal, American Statistical Association
J Am Stud	Journal of American Studies
J Econ Hist	Journal of Economic History
J Hist Ideas	Journal of the History of Ideas
J Mod Hist	Journal of Modern History
J Neg Hist	Journal of Negro History
J Pol	Journal of Politics
J Pol Econ	Journal of Political Economy
J Presby Hist	Journal of Presbyterian History
J S Hist	Journal of Southern History
Jour Q	Journalism Quarterly
Lab Hist	Labor History
Mid-Am	Mid-America
Miss Val Hist Rev	Mississippi Valley Historical Review
N Car Hist Rev	North Carolina Historical Review
N Eng Q	New England Quarterly
Neb Hist	Nebraska History
Pac Hist Rev	Pacific Historical Review
Pol Sci Q	Political Science Quarterly
Proc Acad Pol Sci	Proceedings, Academy of Political Science
Proc Am Philos Soc	Proceedings, American Philosophical Society

ABBREVIATIONS

'Pub Am Jew Hist Soc	Publications, American Jewish Historical Society
Pub Am Stat Assn	Publications, American Statistical Association
Pub Opin Q	Public Opinion Quarterly
Q J Econ	Quarterly Journal of Economics
Rec Am Cath Hist Soc	Records, American Catholic Historical Society
Rev Econ Stat	Review of Economic Statistics
Rev Pol	Review of Politics
S Atl Q	South Atlantic Quarterly
Tech & Cul	Technology and Culture
W Pol Q	Western Political Quarterly
Yale Rev	Yale Review

Note:
Cross-references (**bold face**) are to item numbers. Items marked by a dagger (†) are available in paperback edition at the time this bibliography goes to press. The publisher and compilers invite suggestions for additions to future editions of the bibliography.

I. Bibliographical Guides and Selected Reference Works

1   American Historical Association. *Guide to Historical Literature.* New York, 1961.

2   American Historical Association. *Writings on American History.* 50 vols. Washington, D.C., 1902–1975.

3   BASSETT, T. D. Seymour. "Bibliography: Descriptive and Critical." Vol. II of *Socialism and American Life.* Eds. Donald D. Egbert and Stow Persons. 2 vols. Princeton, 1952.

4   BEMIS, Samuel Flagg, and Grace Gardner GRIFFIN, eds. *Guide to the Diplomatic History of the United States, 1775–1921.* Washington, D.C., 1935.

5   Bureau of the Census. *Historical Statistics of the United States: Colonial Times to 1957.* Washington, D.C., 1960.

6   BURR, Nelson R. "A Critical Bibliography of Religion in America." Vols. III and IV of *Religion in American Life.* Eds. James W. Smith and A. Leland Jamison. 4 vols. Princeton, 1961.†

7   DEXTER, Byron, ed. *The* Foreign Affairs *50–Year Bibliography . . . 1920–1970.* New York, 1972.

8   ELLIS, John Tracy. *A Guide to American Catholic History.* Milwaukee, 1959.

9   FILLER, Louis, ed. *Progressivism and Muckraking: An Interpretive Bibliography.* New York, 1976.

10 FINK, Gary M., *et al.,* eds. *Biographical Dictionary of American Labor Leaders.* Westport, Conn., 1974.

11 FREIDEL, Frank, *et al. Harvard Guide to American History.* Rev. ed. 2 vols. Cambridge, Mass., 1974.

12 GRANTHAM, Dewey W., Jr. "Theodore Roosevelt in American Historical Writing, 1945–1960." *Mid-Am,* XLIV (1961), 3–35.

13 HIGHAM, John, ed. *The Reconstruction of American History.* New York, 1962.

14 JOHNSON, Allen, Dumas MALONE, *et al. Dictionary of American Biography.* 25 vols. New York, 1928–1974.

15 KAPLAN, Louis, ed. *A Bibliography of American Autobiographies.* Madison, Wis., 1961.

16 KUEHL, Warren F., ed. *Dissertations in History: An Index to Dissertations Completed in History Departments of United States and Canadian Universities, 1873–1960.* Lexington, Ky., 1965.

17 LARSON, Henrietta M. *Guide to Business History.* Cambridge, Mass., 1948.

18 Library of Congress. *A Guide to the Study of the United States of America.* Washington, D.C., 1960.

19 LINK, Arthur S., and Rembert W. PATRICK, eds. *Writing Southern History: Essays in Historiography in Honor of Fletcher M. Green.* Baton Rouge, 1965.†

20 MAY, Ernest R. *American Intervention: 1917 and 1941.* Publication no. 30, Service Center for Teachers of History. Washington, D.C., 1960.

21 MC PHERSON, James M., *et al. Blacks in America: Bibliographical Essays.* Garden City, N.Y., 1971.

22 MILLER, Elizabeth W., and Mary FISHER, eds. *The Negro in America: A Bibliography.* Rev. ed. Cambridge, Mass., 1971.†

23 MORRIS, Richard B., ed. *Encyclopedia of American History.* Rev. ed. New York, 1965.

24 MOWRY, George E. *The Progressive Movement, 1900–1920: Recent Ideas and New Literature.* Publication no. 10, Service Center for Teachers of History. New York, 1958.

25 National Research Council, *et al. Doctoral Dissertations Accepted by American Universities. . . .* 22 vols. New York, 1933–1955.

26 NEUFIELD, Maurice F. *A Representative Bibliography of American Labor History.* Ithaca, N.Y., 1964.

27 ROBERTS, Henry L., ed. *Foreign Affairs Bibliography: A Selected and Annotated List of Books on International Relations, 1952–1962.* New York, 1964.

28 SCHLESINGER, Arthur M., Jr., and Fred L. ISRAEL, eds. *History of American Presidential Elections.* 4 vols. New York, 1971.

29 SCHLESINGER, Arthur M., Jr., ed. *History of U.S. Political Parties.* 4 vols. New York, 1973.

30 SPILLER, Robert E., *et al.,* eds. *Literary History of the United States.* Rev. ed. New York, 1963.

31 STROUD, Gene S., and Gilbert E. DONAHUE. *Labor History In the United States: A General Bibliography.* Urbana, Ill., 1961.

32 WATSON, Richard L., Jr. "Woodrow Wilson and His Interpreters, 1947–1957." *Miss Val Hist Rev,* LXIV (1957), 207–236.

33 WOOLBERT, Robert Gale, ed. *Foreign Affairs Bibliography: A Selected and Annotated List of Books on International Relations, 1932–1942.* New York, 1945.

34 Xerox University Microfilms. *Comprehensive Dissertation Index, 1861–1972: History.* Ann Arbor, Mich., 1973.

II. American Politics from Theodore Roosevelt to Woodrow Wilson

1. General

35 BLAISDELL, Thomas C., Jr. *The Federal Trade Commission: An Experiment in the Control of Business.* New York, 1932.

36 BRANDEIS, Elizabeth. "Labor Legislation." *History of Labour in the United States.* Eds. John R. Commons, *et al.* 4 vols. New York, 1918–1935.

37 CHAMBERLAIN, John. *Farewell to Reform.* New York, 1932.†

38 CLARK, John Bates, and John Maurice CLARK. *The Control of Trusts.* New York, 1914.

39 CLARK, John D. *The Federal Trust Policy.* Baltimore, 1931.

40 CUSHMAN, Robert E. "Social and Economic Controls through Federal Taxation." *Minnesota Law Review,* XVIII (1934), 759–783.

41 DORSETT, Lyle W. *The Pendergast Machine.* New York, 1968.†

42 FAINSOD, Merle, and Lincoln GORDON. *Government and the American Economy.* Rev. ed. New York, 1959.

43 FAULKNER, Harold U. *Politics, Reform, and Expansion, 1890–1900.* New York, 1958.

44 FAULKNER, Harold U. *The Quest for Social Justice, 1898–1914.* New York, 1931.†

45 FINE, Sidney. *Laissez Faire and the General Welfare State.* Ann Arbor, Mich., 1956.†

46 FRANKLIN, John Hope. *From Slavery to Freedom: A History of American Negroes.* Rev. ed. New York, 1973.†

47 GINGER, Ray. *Age of Excess: The United States from 1877 to 1914.* 2nd ed. New York, 1975.†

48 GREEN, Marguerite. *The National Civic Federation and the American Labor Movement, 1900–1925.* Washington, D.C., 1956.

49 GRIFFITH, Kathryn. *Judge Learned Hand and the Role of the Federal Judiciary.* Norman, Okla., 1973.

50 HARBESON, Robert W. "Railroads and Regulation, 1877–1916: Conspiracy or Public Interest?" *J Econ Hist,* XXVII (1967), 230–242.

51 HAYS, Samuel P. *The Response to Industrialism, 1885–1914.* Chicago, 1957.†

52 HAYS, Samuel P. "The Social Analysis of American Political History, 1880–1920." *Pol Sci Q,* LXXX (1965), 373–394.

53 HIGHAM, John. *Strangers in the Land: Patterns of American Nativism, 1860–1925.* New Brunswick, N.J., 1955.†

54 HOFSTADTER, Richard. *Age of Reform.* New York, 1955.†

55 HOLLINGSWORTH, J. Rogers. *The Whirligig of Politics: The Democracy of Cleveland and Bryan.* Chicago, 1964.

56 KARSON, Marc. *American Labor Unions and Politics, 1900–1918.* Carbondale, Ill., 1958.

57 KOLKO, Gabriel. *Railroads and Regulation.* Princeton, 1965.†

58 KOLKO, Gabriel. *The Triumph of Conservatism.* New York, 1963.

59 KOUSSER, J. Morgan. *The Shaping of Southern Politics: Suffrage Restriction and the Establishment of the One-Party South, 1880–1910.* New Haven, 1974.

60 LESCOHIER, Don D. "Working Conditions." *History of Labour in the United States.* Eds. John R. Commons, *et al.* 4 vols. New York, 1918–1935.

61 LINK, Arthur S., and William B. CATTON. *American Epoch: A History of the United States Since the 1890s.* 4th ed. New York, 1973.†

62 MILLS, Frederick C. *Economic Tendencies in the United States: Aspects of Pre-War and Post-War Changes.* New York, 1932.

63 MITCHELL, Wesley C. *Business Cycles and Their Causes.* Berkeley, 1941.

64 PERLMAN, Selig, and Philip TAFT. "Labor Movements, 1896–1932." *History of Labour in the United States.* Eds. John R. Commons, *et al.* 4 vols. New York, 1918–1935.

65 RATNER, Sidney. *Taxation and Democracy in America.* New York, 1967. (A revision of *American Taxation.*)

66 SEAGER, Henry R., and Charles A. GULICK. *Trust and Corporation Problems.* New York, 1929.

67 SHARFMAN, I. L. *The Interstate Commerce Commission: A Study in Administrative Law and Procedure.* 4 vols. New York, 1931–1937.

68 SULLIVAN, Mark. *Our Times, 1900–1925.* 6 vols. New York, 1927–1935.

69 TAUSSIG, Frank W. *Tariff History of the United States.* 8th ed. New York, 1931.†

70 THORELLI, Hans B. *The Federal Antitrust Policy.* Stockholm, 1954.

71 TINDALL, George B. *The Emergence of the New South, 1913–1945.* Baton Rouge, 1967.†

72 WATKINS, Myron W. *Industrial Combinations and Public Policy.* Boston, 1957.

73 WIEBE, Robert H. *The Search for Order, 1877–1920.* New York, 1967.†

74 YEARLEY, Clifton K. *The Money Machines: Breakdown and Reform of Governmental and Party Finance in the North, 1860–1920.* Albany, N.Y., 1970.

2. Biographies, Autobiographies, and Collected Works

75 ADDAMS, Jane. *The Second Twenty Years at Hull–House.* New York, 1930.

76 ADDAMS, Jane. *Twenty Years at Hull–House.* New York, 1910.†

77 APTHEKER, Herbert, ed. *The Correspondence of W. E. B. DuBois: Selections, 1877–1934.* Amherst, 1973.

78 BAILEY, Hugh C. *Edward Gardner Murphy: Gentle Progressive.* Coral Gables, 1968.

79 BAKER, Ray Stannard. *American Chronicle.* New York, 1945.

80 BAKER, Ray Stannard. *Woodrow Wilson: Life and Letters.* 8 vols. Garden City, N.Y., 1927–1939.

81 BAKER, Ray Stannard, and William E. DODD, eds. *The Public Papers of Woodrow Wilson.* 6 vols. New York, 1925–1927.

82 BANNISTER, Robert C., Jr. *Ray Stannard Baker: The Mind and Thought of a Progressive.* New Haven, 1966.

83 BARKER, Charles A. *Henry George.* New York, 1955.

84 BELL, Herbert C. F. *Woodrow Wilson and the People.* Garden City, N.Y., 1945.

85 BILLINGTON, Monroe Lee. *Thomas P. Gore.* Lawrence, Kan., 1967.

86 BLUM, John M. *Joe Tumulty and the Wilson Era.* Boston, 1951.

87 BLUM, John M. *Woodrow Wilson and the Politics of Morality.* Boston, 1956.†

88 BLUMBERG, Dorothy Rose. *Florence Kelley: The Making of a Social Pioneer.* New York, 1966.

89 BOWERS, Claude G. *Beveridge and the Progressive Era.* New York, 1932.

90 BRAEMAN, John. *Albert J. Beveridge: American Nationalist.* Chicago, 1971.

91 BRAGDON, Henry W. *Woodrow Wilson: The Academic Years.* Cambridge, Mass., 1967.

92 BRODERICK, Francis L. *W. E. B. DuBois: Negro Leader in a Time of Crisis.* Stanford, 1959.†

93 BROESAMLE, John J. *William Gibbs McAdoo: A Passion for Change.* Port Washington, N.Y., 1973.

94 BROOKS, Aubrey L., and Hugh T. LEFLER, eds. *The Papers of Walter Clark.* 2 vols. Chapel Hill, 1948–1949.

95 BRYAN, Mary B., ed. *The Memoirs of William Jennings Bryan.* Philadelphia, 1925.

96 BUTT, Archibald W. *Taft and Roosevelt: The Intimate Letters of Archie Butt, Military Aide.* 2 vols. Garden City, N.Y., 1930.

97 CHESSMAN, G. Wallace. *Theodore Roosevelt and the Politics of Power.* Boston, 1968.†

98 COBEN, Stanley. *A. Mitchell Palmer: Politician.* New York, 1963.

99 COHEN, Naomi W. *A Dual Heritage: The Public Career of Oscar Straus.* Philadelphia, 1969.

100 COIT, Margaret L. *Mr. Baruch.* Boston, 1957.

101 COLETTA, Paola E. *William Jennings Bryan.* 3 vols. Lincoln, Neb., 1964–1969.

102 COMMONS, John R. *Myself.* New York, 1934.†

103 CRAMER, Clarence H. *Newton D. Baker.* Cleveland, 1961.

104 CREEL, George. *Rebel at Large.* New York, 1947.

105 CROLY, Herbert D. *Marcus Alonzo Hanna.* New York, 1912.

106 CRONON, E. David, ed. *The Cabinet Diaries of Josephus Daniels, 1913–1921.* Lincoln, Neb., 1963.

107 CRUNDEN, Robert M. *A Hero in Spite of Himself: Brand Whitlock in Art, Politics, & War.* New York, 1969.

108 DANIELS, Josephus. *Editor in Politics.* Chapel Hill, 1941.

109 DANIELS, Josephus. *Tar Heel Editor.* Chapel Hill, 1939.

110 DANIELS, Josephus. *The Wilson Era.* 2 vols. Chapel Hill, 1944–1946.

111 DAVIS, Allen F. *American Heroine: The Life & Legend of Jane Addams.* New York, 1973.†

112 ELLIS, Elmer. *Mr. Dooley's America: A Life of Finley Peter Dunne.* New York, 1941.

113 ELY, Richard T. *Ground Under Our Feet.* New York, 1938.

114 FAUSOLD, Martin L. *James W. Wadsworth, Jr.: The Gentleman from New York.* Syracuse, N.Y., 1975.

115 FLYNT, Wayne. *Duncan Upshaw Fletcher: Dixie's Reluctant Progressive.* Tallahassee, 1971.

116 FOWLER, Dorothy. *John Coit Spooner.* New York, 1961.

117 FREIDEL, Frank. *Franklin D. Roosevelt: The Apprenticeship.* Boston, 1952.

118 GARRATY, John A. *Henry Cabot Lodge.* New York, 1953.

119 GARRATY, John A. *Right-Hand Man: The Life of George W. Perkins.* New York, 1960.

120 GARRATY, John A. *Woodrow Wilson.* New York, 1956.

121 GARRATY, John A. "Woodrow Wilson: A Study in Personality." *S Atl Q,* LVI (1957), 176–85.

122 GEIGER, Louis G. *Joseph W. Folk of Missouri.* Columbia, Mo., 1953.†

123 GEORGE, Alexander L., and Juliette L. GEORGE. *Woodrow Wilson and Colonel House: A Personality Study.* New York, 1956.†

124 GINGER, Ray. *The Bending Cross: A Biography of Eugene Victor Debs.* New Brunswick, N.J., 1949.†

125 GLAD, Paul W. *The Trumpet Soundeth: William Jennings Bryan and His Democracy, 1896–1912.* Lincoln, Neb., 1960.†

126 GOLDMARK, Josephine C. *Impatient Crusader: Florence Kelley's Life Story.* Urbana, Ill., 1953.

127 GOMPERS, Samuel. *Seventy Years of Life and Labor: An Autobiography.* 2 vols. New York, 1925.

128 GOTTFRIED, Alex. *Boss Cermak of Chicago.* Seattle, 1962.

129 GRANTHAM, Dewey W., Jr. *Hoke Smith and the Politics of the New South.* Baton Rouge, 1958.†

130 GRAYBAR, Lloyd J. *Albert Shaw of the* Review of Reviews*: An Intellectual Biography.* Lexington, Ky., 1974.

131 GRAYSON, Cary T. *Woodrow Wilson: An Intimate Memoir.* New York, 1960.

132 GREENBAUM, Fred. *Fighting Progressive: A Biography of Edward P. Costigan.* Washington, D.C., 1971.

133 GREGORY, Ross. *Walter Hines Page: Ambassador to the Court of St. James's.* Lexington, Ky., 1970.

134 GWINN, William Rea. *Uncle Joe Cannon, Archfoe of Insurgency.* New York, 1957.

135 HAGEDORN, Hermann. *Leonard Wood.* 2 vols. New York, 1931.

136 HAGEDORN, Hermann. *The Roosevelt Family of Sagamore Hill.* New York, 1954.

137 HARBAUGH, William H. *Lawyer's Lawyer: The Life of John W. Davis.* New York, 1973.

138 HARBAUGH, William H. *Power and Responsibility: The Life and Times of Theodore Roosevelt.* New York, 1961.†

6

139 HARLAN, Louis R. *Booker T. Washington: The Making of a Black Leader, 1856–1901.* New York, 1972.†

140 HARLAN, Louis R., *et al.,* eds. *The Booker T. Washington Papers.* 4 vols. Urbana, Ill., 1973–1975.

141 HARRIS, Leon. *Upton Sinclair: American Rebel.* New York, 1975.

142 HELMES, Winifred G. *John A. Johnson: the People's Governor.* Minneapolis, 1949.

143 HENDRICK, Burton J. *The Life of Andrew Carnegie.* 2 vols. New York, 1932.

144 HENDRICK, Burton J. *The Life and Letters of Walter H. Page.* 3 vols. Garden City, N.Y., 1922–1925.

145 HOLMES, William F. *The White Chief: James Kimble Vardaman.* Baton Rouge, 1970.

146 HOUSTON, David F. *Eight Years with Wilson's Cabinet, 1913 to 1920.* 2 vols. Garden City, N.Y., 1926.

147 HOWE, Frederic C. *The Confessions of a Reformer.* New York, 1925.†

148 HOWE, M. A. DeWolfe. *George von Lengerke Meyer.* New York, 1920.

149 HUTCHINSON, William T. *Lowden of Illinois.* 2 vols. Chicago, 1957.†

150 HUTHMACHER, J. Joseph. *Senator Robert F. Wagner and the Rise of Urban Liberalism.* New York, 1968.†

151 JESSUP, Philip C. *Elihu Root.* 2 vols. New York, 1938.

152 JOHNSON, Tom L. *My Story.* New York, 1911.

153 JOHNSON, Walter. *William Allen White's America.* New York, 1947.

154 KAPLAN, Justin. *Lincoln Steffens.* New York, 1974.

155 KERNEY, James. *The Political Education of Woodrow Wilson.* New York, 1926.

156 KURLAND, Gerald. *Seth Low: The Reformer in an Urban and Industrial Age.* New York, 1971.

157 LA FOLLETTE, Belle C. and Fola LA FOLLETTE. *Robert M. La Follette.* 2 vols. New York, 1953.

158 LAMBERT, John R. *Arthur Pue Gorman.* Baton Rouge, 1953.

159 LAMBERT, Oscar D. *Stephen Benton Elkins.* Pittsburgh, 1955.

160 LANE, Anne W., and Louise H. WALL, eds. *The Letters of Franklin K. Lane, Personal and Political.* Boston, 1922.

161 LARSEN, Charles. *The Good Fight: The Life and Times of Ben B. Lindsey.* Chicago, 1972.

162 LARSEN, William. *Montague of Virginia: The Making of a Southern Progressive.* Baton Rouge, 1965.

163 LARSON, Bruce L. *Lindbergh of Minnesota: A Political Biography.* New York, 1973.

164 LEOPOLD, Richard W. *Elihu Root and the Conservative Tradition.* Boston, 1954.†

165 LEVINE, Daniel. *Jane Addams and the Liberal Tradition.* Madison, Wis., 1971.

166 LEVINE, Lawrence W. *Defender of the Faith: William Jennings Bryan; the Last Decade, 1915–1925.* New York, 1965.†

167 LINK, Arthur S., *et al.*, eds. *The Papers of Woodrow Wilson.* 24 vols. to date. Princeton, 1966–.

168 LINK, Arthur S. *Wilson: Campaigns for Progressivism and Peace, 1916–1917.* Princeton, 1965.

169 LINK, Arthur S. *Wilson: Confusions and Crises, 1915–1916.* Princeton, 1964.

170 LINK, Arthur S. *Wilson: The New Freedom.* Princeton, 1956.

171 LINK, Arthur S. *Wilson: The Road to the White House.* Princeton, 1947.†

172 LINK, Arthur S. *Wilson: The Struggle for Neutrality, 1914–1915.* Princeton, 1960.

173 LINK, Arthur S. *Woodrow Wilson: A Brief Biography.* Cleveland, 1963.†

174 LINN, James Weber. *Jane Addams.* New York, 1935.

175 LOWITT, Richard. *George W. Norris: The Making of a Progressive, 1861–1912.* Syracuse, N.Y., 1963.

176 LOWITT, Richard. *George W. Norris: The Persistence of a Progressive, 1913–1933.* Urbana, Ill. 1971.

177 MANDELL, Bernard. *Samuel Gompers: A Biography.* Yellow Springs, Ohio, 1963.

178 MANN, Arthur. *La Guardia: A Fighter Against his Times, 1882–1933.* Philadelphia, 1959.†

179 MARTIN, Abro. *James J. Hill and the Opening of the Northwest.* New York, 1976.

180 MASON, Alpheus T. *Brandeis: A Free Man's Life.* New York, 1946.

181 MAXWELL, Robert S. *Emanuel L. Philipp: Wisconsin Stalwart.* Madison, Wis., 1959.

182 MC ADOO, William G. *Crowded Years: The Reminiscences of William G. McAdoo.* Boston, 1931.

183 MC GEARY, M. Nelson. *Gifford Pinchot: Forester–Politician.* Princeton, 1960.

184 MC KEE, John D. *William Allen White: Maverick on Main Street.* Westport, Conn., 1975.

185 MORISON, Elting E. *Turmoil and Tradition: A Study of the Life and Times of Henry L. Stimson.* Boston, 1960.

186 MORISON, Elting E. and John M. BLUM, eds. *The Letters of Theodore Roosevelt.* 8 vols. Cambridge, Mass., 1951–1954.

187 NEVINS, Allan. *The Letters and Journal of Brand Whitlock.* 2 vols. New York, 1936.

188 NORRIS, George W. *Fighting Liberal: The Autobiography of George W. Norris.* New York, 1945.†

189 O'BRIEN, Francis W., ed. *The Hoover-Wilson Wartime Correspondence, September 24, 1914 to November 11, 1918.* Ames, Iowa, 1974.

190 OLDER, Fremont. *William Randolph Hearst.* New York, 1936.

191 ORR, Oliver H., Jr. *Charles Brantley Aycock.* Chapel Hill, 1961.

192 OSBORN, George C. *John Sharp Williams.* Baton Rouge, 1943.

193 OSBORN, George C. *Woodrow Wilson: The Early Years.* Baton Rouge, 1968.

194 PALMER, Frederick. *Newton D. Baker.* 2 vols. New York, 1931.

195 PERKINS, Dexter. *Charles Evans Hughes and American Democratic Statesmanship.* Boston, 1956.

196 PINKETT, Harold T. *Gifford Pinchot: Private and Public Forester.* Urbana, Ill., 1970.

197 PRINGLE, Henry F. *The Life and Times of William Howard Taft.* 2 vols. New York, 1939.

198 PRINGLE, Henry F. *Theodore Roosevelt.* New York, 1931.†

199 PUSEY, Merlo J. *Charles Evans Hughes.* 2 vols. New York, 1951.

200 ROOSEVELT, Theodore. *An Autobiography.* New York, 1919.

201 *The Works of Theodore Roosevelt.* 20 vols. (National edition.) New York, 1926.

202 ROPER, Daniel C. *Fifty Years of Public Life.* Durham, N.C., 1941.

203 ROSENSTONE, Robert A. *Romantic Revolutionary: A Biography of John Reed.* New York, 1975.

204 ROSS, Edward A. *Seventy Years of It.* New York, 1936.

205 SAGE, Leland L. *William Boyd Allison: A Study in Practical Politics.* Iowa City, 1956.

206 SAGESER, A. Bower. *John L. Bristow: Kansas Progressive.* Lawrence, Kan., 1968.

207 SEMONCHE, John E. *Ray Stannard Baker: A Quest for Democracy in Modern America, 1870–1918.* Chapel Hill, 1969.

208 SEYMOUR, Charles. *The Intimate Papers of Colonel House.* 4 vols. Boston, 1926–1928.

209 SIMKINS, Francis B. *Pitchfork Ben Tillman, South Carolinian.* Baton Rouge, 1944.†

210 SMITH, Rixey, and Norman BEASLEY. *Carter Glass.* New York, 1939.

211 SMYTHE, Donald. *Guerrilla Warrior: The Early Life of John J. Pershing.* New York, 1973.

212 STEFFENS, Lincoln. *The Autobiography of Lincoln Steffens.* New York, 1931.†

213 STEPHENSON, George M. *John Lind of Minnesota.* Minneapolis, 1935.

214 STEPHENSON, Nathaniel W. *Nelson W. Aldrich.* New York, 1930.

215 SULLIVAN, Mark. *The Education of an American.* New York, 1938.

216 SWANBERG, W. A. *Citizen Hearst.* New York, 1961.

217 SWANBERG, W. A. *Pulitzer.* New York, 1967.

218 TARR, Joel A. *A Study in Boss Politics: William Lorimer of Chicago.* Urbana, Ill., 1971.

219 THELEN, David P. *Robert M. La Follette and the Insurgent Spirit.* Boston, 1976.†

220 UROFSKY, Melvin I., and David W. LEVY, eds. *Letters of Louis D. Brandeis.* 4 vols. Albany, N.Y., 1971–1975.

221 VANCE, Maurice M. *Charles Richard Van Hise: Scientist Progressive.* Madison, Wis., 1960.

222 VILLARD, Osward Garrison. *Fighting Years: Memoirs of a Liberal Editor.* New York, 1939.

223 WADE, Louise C. *Graham Taylor: Pioneer for Social Justice, 1851–1938.* Chicago, 1964.

224 WALD, Lillian D. *The House on Henry Street.* New York, 1915.†

225 WALWORTH, Arthur. *Woodrow Wilson.* 2 vols. New York, 1958.

226 WASHINGTON, Booker T. *Up From Slavery.* New York, 1901.†

227 WATTERSON, Henry. *"Marse Henry:" An Autobiography.* 2 vols. New York, 1919.

228 WEISS, Nancy J. *Charles Francis Murphy, 1858–1924: Respectability and Responsibility in Tammany Politics.* Northampton, Mass., 1968.

229 WHITE, William Allen. *The Autobiography of William Allen White.* New York, 1946.

230 WINTER, Ella, and Granville HICKS, eds. *The Letters of Lincoln Steffens.* 2 vols. New York, 1938.

231 WOODWARD, C. Vann. *Tom Watson: Agrarian Rebel.* New York, 1938.†

232 WRESZIN, Michael. *The Superfluous Anarchist: Albert Jay Nock.* Providence, R.I., 1972.

233 ZUCKER, Norman L. *George W. Norris: Gentle Knight of American Democracy.* Urbana, Ill., 1966.

3. The Progressive Movement

A. General

234 ALLEN, Howard W. "Geography and Politics: Voting on Reform Issues in the United States Senate, 1911–1916." *J S Hist,* XXVII (1961), 216–28.

235 ALLEN, Howard W., and Jerome CLUBB. "Progressive Reform and the Political System." *Pacific Northwest Quarterly,* LXV (1974), 130–45.

236 BOWERS, Claude G. *Beveridge and the Progressive Era.* See **89.**

237 BRAEMAN, John. "Seven Progressives." *Bus Hist Rev,* XXXV (1961), 581–92.

238 BROOKS, Aubrey L., and Hugh T. LEFLER, eds. *The Papers of Walter Clark.* See **94.**

239 BRYAN, Mary B., ed. *The Memoirs of William Jennings Bryan.* See **95.**

240 BUENKER, John D. "The Progressive Era: A Search for a Synthesis." *Mid-Am,* LI (1969), 175–93.

241 BUENKER, John D. *Urban Liberalism and Progressive Reform.* New York, 1973.

242 CHAMBERLAIN, John. *Farewell to Reform.* See **37.**

243 COLETTA, Paola E. *William Jennings Bryan.* See **101.**

244 CUTLIP, Scott M. *Fund Raising in the United States: Its Role in America's Philanthropy.* New Brunswick, N.J., 1965.

245 DANIELS, Josephus. *Editor in Politics.* See **108.**

246 DANIELS, Josephus. *Tar Heel Editor.* See **109.**

247 DE WITT, Benjamin Parke. *The Progressive Movement.* New York, 1915.

248 ELY, Richard T. *Ground Under Our Feet.* See **113.**

249 FILENE, Peter G. "An Obituary for 'The Progressive Movement.' " *Am Q,* XXII (1970), 20–34.

250 FLEXNER, Eleanor. *Century of Struggle: The Woman's Rights Movement in the United States.* Cambridge, Mass., 1959.†

251 GLAD, Paul W. *The Trumpet Soundeth.* See **125.**

252 GOULD, Lewis L., ed. *The Progressive Era.* Syracuse, N.Y., 1974.†

253 GRAHAM, Otis L., Jr. *The Great Campaigns: Reform and War in America, 1900–1928.* Englewood Cliffs, N.J., 1971.†

254 GRANTHAM, Dewey W., Jr. "The Progressive Era and the Reform Tradition." *Mid-Am,* XLVI (1964), 227–51.

255 HABER, Samuel. *Efficiency and Uplift: Scientific Management in the Progressive Era, 1890–1920.* Chicago, 1964.

256 HILLJE, John W. "The Progressive Movement and the Graduated Income Tax, 1913–1919." Doctoral dissertation, University of Texas, 1966.

257 HOFSTADTER, Richard. *Age of Reform.* See **54.**

258 HOWE, Frederic C. *The Confessions of a Reformer.* See **147.**

259 JACK, Robert L. *History of the National Association for the Advancement of Colored People.* Boston, 1943.

260 KELLOGG, Charles Flint. *NAACP: A History of the National Association for the Advancement of Colored People, 1909–1920.* Baltimore, 1967.†

261 KELLOGG, Paul Underwood, ed. *The Pittsburgh Survey.* 6 vols. New York, 1909–1914.

262 KENNEDY, David M. "Overview: The Progressive Era." *Historian,* XXXVII (1975), 453–68.

263 KOLKO, Gabriel. *The Triumph of Conservatism.* See **58.**

264 KRADITOR, Aileen S. *The Ideas of the Woman Suffrage Movement, 1890–1920.* New York, 1965.†

265 LEVINE, Daniel. *Varieties of Reform Thought.* Madison, Wis., 1964.†

266 MADISON, Charles A. *Leaders and Liberals in 20th Century America.* New York, 1961.

267 MARCHAND, C. Roland. *The American Peace Movement and Social Reform, 1898–1918.* Princeton, 1973.

268 MARTIN, Albro. *Enterprise Denied: Origins of the Decline of American Railroads, 1897–1917.* New York, 1971.

269 MASON, Alpheus T. *Brandeis.* See **180.**

270 MORRIS, Stuart. "The Wisconsin Idea and Business Progressivism." *J Am Stud,* IV (1970), 39–60.

271 ODEGARD, Peter H. *Pressure Politics: The Story of the Anti-Saloon League.* New York, 1928

272 SEMONCHE, John E. *Ray Stannard Baker.* See **207.**

273 SOUTHERN, David W. *The Malignant Heritage: Yankee Progressives and the Negro Question, 1901–1914.* Chicago, 1968.

274 TAGER, Jack. "Progressives, Conservatives, and the Theory of Status Revolution." *Mid-Am,* XLVIII (1966), 162–75.

275 THELEN, David P. *Robert M. La Follette.* See **219.**

276 THELEN, David P. "Social Tensions and the Origins of Progressivism." *J Am Hist,* LVI (1969), 323–41.

277 TIMBERLAKE, James H. *Prohibition and the Progressive Movement, 1900–1920.* Cambridge, Mass., 1963.†

278 UROFSKY, Melvin I., and David W. LEVY, eds. *Letters of Louis D. Brandeis.* See **220.**

279 WIEBE, Robert H. *Businessmen and Reform: A Study of the Progressive Movement.* Cambridge, Mass., 1962.†

B. Progressivism in the Cities and States

280 ABRAMS, Richard M. *Conservatism in a Progressive Era: Massachusetts Politics, 1900–1912.* Cambridge, Mass., 1964.

281 ABRAMS, Richard M. "A Paradox of Progressivism: Massachusetts on the Eve of Insurgency." *Pol Sci Q,* LXXV (1960), 373–99.

282 BACON, Charles Reade. *A People Awakened.* Garden City, N.Y., 1912.

283 BAILEY, Hugh C. *Edgar Gardner Murphy.* See **78.**

284 BARR, Alwyn. *Reconstruction to Reform: Texas Politics, 1876–1906.* Austin, 1971.

285 BEAN, Walton E. *Boss Ruef's San Francisco.* Berkeley, 1952.†

286 BLACKFORD, Mansel G. "Reform Politics in Seattle during the Progressive Era, 1902–1916." *Pacific Northwest Quarterly,* LIX (1959), 177–85.

287 BUENKER, John D. *Urban Liberalism and Progressive Reform.* See **241.**

288 BUENKER, John D. "The Urban Political Machine and the Seventeenth Amendment." *J Am Hist,* LVI (1969), 305–22.

289 BURTS, Robert M. *Richard Irvine Manning and the Progressive Movement in South Carolina.* Columbia, S.C., 1974.

290 CAINE, Stanley P. *The Myth of a Progressive Reform: Railroad Regulation in Wisconsin, 1903–1910.* Madison, Wis., 1970.

291 CAINE, Stanley P. "Why Railroads Supported Regulation: The Case of Wisconsin, 1905–1910." *Bus Hist Rev,* XLIV (1970), 175–89.

292 CHRISLOCK, Carl H. *The Progressive Era in Minnesota, 1899–1918.* St. Paul, Minn., 1971.

293 CROOKS, James B. *Politics and Progress: The Rise of Urban Progressivism in Baltimore, 1895–1911.* Baton Rouge, 1968.

294 CROW, Jeffrey J. "Populism to Progressivism in North Carolina: Governor Daniel Russell and His War on the Southern Railway Company." *Historian,* XXXVII (1975), 649–67.

295 DOHERTY, Herbert J., Jr. "Voices of Protest from the New South, 1875-1910." *Miss Val Hist Rev,* XLII (1955), 45-66.

296 DUBOFSKY, Melvyn. *When Workers Organize: New York City in the Progressive Era.* Amherst, Mass., 1968.

297 FERRELL, Henry C., Jr. "Prohibition, Reform, and Politics in Virginia, 1895-1916." *East Carolina College Publications in History,* III (1966), 175-42.

298 FLINT, Winston Allen. *The Progressive Movement in Vermont.* Washington, D.C., 1941.

299 FLYNT, Wayne. *Duncan Upshaw Fletcher.* See **115.**

300 GEIGER, Louis G. *Joseph W. Folk of Missouri.* See **122.**

301 GIST, Genevieve B. "Progressive Reform in a Rural Community: The Adams County [Ohio] Vote-Fraud Case." *Miss Val Hist Rev,* XLVIII (1961), 60-78.

302 GLAAB, Charles N. "The Failure of North Dakota Progressivism." *Mid-Am,* XXXIX (1957), 195-209.

303 GOTTFRIED, Alex. *Boss Cermak of Chicago.* See **128.**

304 GOULD, Lewis L. *Progressives and Prohibitionists: Texas Democrats in the Wilson Era.* Austin, 1973.†

305 GRANTHAM, Dewey W., Jr. *Hoke Smith and the Politics of the New South.* See **129.**

306 GREEN, Constance. *Washington: Capital City, 1879-1950.* Princeton, 1953.†

307 GREEN, Fletcher M. "Some Aspects of the Convict Lease System in the Southern States." *Essays in Southern History Presented to Joseph Gregoire de Roulhac Hamilton. . . .* Ed. Fletcher M. Green. Chapel Hill, 1949.

308 GREENBAUM, Fred. *Fighting Progressive: A Biography of Edward P. Costigan.* Washington, D.C., 1971.

309 GRIFFITH, Ernest S. *A History of American City Government: The Progressive Years and Their Aftermath, 1900-1920.* New York, 1974.

310 HACKNEY, Sheldon. *Populism to Progressivism in Alabama.* Princeton, 1969.

311 HAYS, Samuel P. "The Politics of Reform in Municipal Government in the Progressive Era." *Pacific Northwest Quarterly,* LV (1964), 157-69.

312 HEATH, Frederick M. "Labor and the Progressive Movement in Connecticut." *Lab Hist,* XII (1971), 52-67.

313 HELMES, Winifred G. *John A. Johnson: the People's Governor.* See **142.**

314 HIRST, David W., ed. *Woodrow Wilson: Reform Governor.* Princeton, 1965.

315 HOLLI, Melvin G. *Reform in Detroit: Hazen S. Pingree and Urban Politics.* New York, 1969.†

316 HUTHMACHER, J. Joseph. *Senator Robert F. Wagner and the Rise of Urban Liberalism.* See **150.**

317 HUTHMACHER, J. Joseph. "Urban Liberalism and the Age of Reform." *Miss Val Hist Rev,* XLIX (1962), 231-41.

318 ISSAC, Paul E. *Prohibition and Politics: Turbulent Decades in Tennessee, 1885-1920.* Knoxville, 1965.

319 JANICK, Herbert. "The Mind of the Connecticut Progressive." *Mid-Am,* LII (1970), 83-101.

320 JOHNSON, Tom L. *My Story.* See **152.**

321 KERR, William T., Jr. "The Progressives in Washington, 1910–1920." *Pacific Northwest Quarterly,* LV (1964), 16–27.

322 KIRWAN, Albert D. *The Revolt of the Rednecks: Mississippi Politics, 1876–1925.* Lexington, Ky., 1951.

323 KURLAND, Gerald. *Seth Low.* See **156.**

234 LA FORTE, Robert S. *Leaders of Reform: Progressive Republicans in Kansas, 1900–1916.* Lawrence, Kan., 1974.

325 LARSEN, Charles. *The Good Fight: The Life and Times of Ben B. Lindsey.* See **161.**

326 LARSEN, William. *Montague of Virginia.* See **162.**

327 LINK, Arthur S. "The Progressive Movement in the South, 1870–1914." *N Car Hist Rev,* XXIII (1946), 172–95.

328 LOWITT, Richard. *George W. Norris.* See **176.**

329 MANN, Arthur. *Yankee Reformers in the Urban Age.* Cambridge, Mass., 1954.†

330 MARGULIES, Herbert F. *The Decline of the Progressive Movement in Wisconsin, 1890–1920.* Madison, Wis., 1968.

331 MAXWELL, Robert S. *Emanuel L. Philipp.* See **181.**

332 MAXWELL, Robert S. *La Follette and the Rise of Progressives in Wisconsin.* Madison, Wis., 1956.

333 MC KELVEY, Blake. *Rochester: The Quest for Quality, 1890–1925.* Cambridge, Mass., 1956.

334 MILLER, William D. *Memphis during the Progressive Era, 1900–1917.* Memphis, 1957.

335 MILLER, Zane L. *Boss Cox's Cincinnati: Urban Politics in the Progressive Era.* New York, 1968.†

336 MOGER, Allen W. *Virginia: Bourbonism to Byrd, 1870–1925.* Charlottesville, Va., 1968.

337 MOWRY, George E. "The California Progressive and His Rationale: A Study in Middle Class Politics." *Miss Val Hist Rev,* XXXVI (1949), 239–50.

338 MOWRY, George E. *The California Progressives.* Berkeley, 1951.†

339 NELLI, Humbert S. "John Powers and the Italians: Politics in a Chicago Ward, 1896–1921." *J Am Hist,* LVII (1970), 67–84.

340 NOBLE, Ransom E., Jr. *New Jersey Progressivism Before Wilson.* Princeton, 1946.

341 NORRIS, George W. *Fighting Liberal.* See **188.**

342 NYE, Russel B. *Midwestern Progressive Politics.* East Lansing, Mich., 1951.

343 OLIN, Spencer C., Jr. *California's Prodigal Sons: Hiram Johnson and the Progressives, 1911–1917.* Berkeley, 1968.

344 ORR, Oliver H., Jr. *Charles Brantley Aycock.* See **191.**

345 OSBORN, George C. *John Sharp Williams.* See **192.**

346 OSTRANDER, Gilman M. *The Prohibition Movement in California, 1848–1933.* Berkeley, 1957.

347 POTTS, E. Daniel. "The Progressive Profile in Iowa." *Mid-Am,* XLVII (1965), 257–68.

348 PULLEY, Raymond H. *Old Virginia Restored: An Interpretation of the Progressive Impulse, 1870–1930.* Charlottesville, Va., 1968.

349 PUSEY, Merlo J. *Charles Evans Hughes.* See **199.**

350 REYNOLDS, George M. *Machine Politics in New Orleans, 1897–1926.* New York, 1936.

351 RINGENBACH, Paul T. *Tramps and Reformers, 1873–1916: The Discovery of Unemployment in New York.* Westport, Conn., 1973.

352 ROSENBERG, Arnold S. "The New York Reformers of 1914: A Profile." *New York History,* L (1969), 187–206.

353 SAGESER, A. Bower. *John L. Bristow.* See **206.**

354 SAXTON, Alexander. "San Francisco Labor and Populist and Progressive Insurgencies." *Pac Hist Rev,* XXXIV (1965), 421–38.

355 SELLERS, James B. *The Prohibition Movement in Alabama, 1702 to 1943.* Chapel Hill, 1943.†

356 SHERMAN, Richard B. "The Status Revolution and Massachusetts Progressive Leadership." *Pol Sci Q,* LXXVIII (1963), 59–65.

357 SHOVER, John L. "The Progressives and the Working Class Vote in California." *Lab Hist,* X (1969), 584–601.

358 STAPLES, Henry L., and Alpheus T. MASON. *The Fall of a Railroad Empire: Brandeis and the New Haven Merger Battle.* Syracuse, N.Y., 1947.

359 STEELMAN, Joseph F. "The Progressive Era in North Carolina, 1884–1917." Doctoral dissertation, University of North Carolina, 1955.

360 STEELMAN, Joseph F. "Progressivism and Agitation for Legal Reform in North Carolina, 1897–1917." *East Carolina College Publications in History,* I (1964), 94–164.

361 STEFFENS, Lincoln. *The Shame of the Cities.* New York, 1904.†

362 STEFFENS, Lincoln. *The Struggle for Self-Government.* New York, 1906.

363 STEPHENSON, George M. *John Lind of Minnesota.* See **213.**

364 STEWART, Frank M. *A Half-Century of Municipal Reform: The History of the National Municipal League.* Berkeley, 1950.

365 TAGER, Jack. *The Intellectual as Urban Reformer: Brand Whitlock and the Progressive Movement.* Cleveland, 1968.

366 TAYLOR, A. Elizabeth. *The Woman Suffrage Movement in Tennessee.* New York, 1957.

367 THELEN, David P. *The New Citizenship: Origins of Progressivism in Wisconsin, 1885–1900.* Columbia, Mo., 1972.

368 THELEN, David P. *Robert M. La Follette.* See **219.**

369 TINSLEY, James A. "The Progressive Movement in Texas." Doctoral dissertation, University of Wisconsin, 1954.

370 WARNER, Hoyt Landon. *Progressivism in Ohio, 1897–1917.* Columbus, Ohio, 1964.

371 WEINSTEIN, James. "Organized Business and the City Commission and Manager Movements." *J S Hist*, XXVIII (1962), 166–82.

372 WEISS, Nancy J. *Charles Francis Murphy*. See **228.**

373 WESSER, Robert F. *Charles Evans Hughes: Politics and Reform in New York, 1905–1910.* Ithaca, N.Y., 1967.

374 WHITENER, Daniel J. *Prohibition in North Carolina, 1715–1945.* Chapel Hill, 1946.

375 WOODWARD, C. Vann. *Origins of the New South, 1877–1913.* Baton Rouge, 1951.†

376 YELLOWITZ, Irwin. *Labor and Progressive Movement in New York State, 1897–1916.* Ithaca, N.Y., 1965.

377 ZINK, Harold. *City Bosses in the United States.* Durham, N.C., 1930.

378 ZUCKER, Norman L. *George W. Norris.* See **233.**

C. The Social Justice Movement

379 ADDAMS, Jane. *The Second Twenty Years at Hull–House.* See **75.**

380 ADDAMS, Jane. *Twenty Years at Hull–House.* See **76.**

381 ASHER, Robert. "Business and Workers' Welfare in the Progressive Era: Workmen's Compensation Reform in Massachusetts, 1880–1911." *Bus Hist Rev*, XLIII (1969), 452–75.

382 ATHEY, Louis L. "Florence Kelley and the Quest for Negro Equality." *J Neg Hist*, LVI (1971), 249–61.

383 BEARDSLEY, Edward H. "The American Scientist as Social Activist: Franz Boas, Bart S. Wilder, and the Case of Racial Justice, 1900–1915." *Isis*, LXIV (1973), 50–66.

384 BLUMBERG, Dorothy R. *Florence Kelley.* See **88.**

385 BREMNER, Robert H. *American Philanthropy.* Chicago, 1960.†

386 BREMNER, Robert H. "The Big Flat: History of a New York Tenement House." *Am Hist Rev*, LXIV (1958), 54–62.

387 BREMNER, Robert H. *From the Depths: The Discovery of Poverty in the United States.* New York, 1956.†

388 BRUNO, Frank, Jr., and Louis TOWLEY. *Trends in Social Work, 1874–1956.* New York, 1957.

389 BRYANT, Keith L., Jr. "Kate Barnard, Organized Labor, and Social Justice in Oklahoma during the Progressive Era." *J S Hist*, XXXV (1969), 145–64.

390 CHAMBERS, Clarke A. *Paul U. Kellogg and the Survey: Voices for Social Welfare and Social Justice.* Minneapolis, 1971.

391 CHAMBERS, Clarke A. *Seedtime of Reform: American Social Service and Social Action, 1918–1933.* Minneapolis, 1963.

392 DAVIDSON, Elizabeth H. *Child Labor Legislation in the Southern Textile States.* Chapel Hill, 1939.

393 DAVIS, Allen F. *American Heroine.* See **111.**

394 DAVIS, Allen F. "Settlement Workers in Politics, 1890–1914." *Rev Pol,* XXVI (1964), 505–17.

395 DAVIS, Allen F. "The Social Workers and the Progressive Party, 1912–1916." *Am Hist Rev,* LXIX (1964), 671–88.

396 DAVIS, Allen F. *Spearheads for Reform: The Social Settlements and the Progressive Movement, 1890–1914.* New York, 1967.†

397 DERBER, Milton. "The Idea of Industrial Democracy in America, 1898–1915." *Lab Hist,* VII (1966), 259–86.

398 EASTMAN, Crystal. *Work-Accidents and the Law.* New York, 1910.

399 FELT, Jeremy P. *Hostages of Fortune: Child Labor Reform in New York State.* Syracuse, N.Y., 1965.

400 GOLDMARK, Josephine C. *Impatient Crusader.* See **126.**

401 GREER, Thomas H. *American Social Reform Movements: Their Pattern Since 1865.* New York, 1949.

402 HOLDEN, Arthur C. *The Settlement Idea.* New York, 1922.

403 HOLL, Jack M. *Juvenile Reform in the Progressive Era: William R. George and the Junior Republican Movement.* Ithaca, N.Y., 1971.

404 HOWE, Frederic C. *The Confessions of a Reformer.* See **147.**

405 KERR, Thomas J., IV. "The New York Factory Investigating Commission and the Minimum Wage Movement." *Lab Hist,* XII (1971), 373–91.

406 KUSMER, Kenneth L. "The Functions of Organized Charity in the Progressive Era: Chicago as a Case Study." *J Am Hist,* LX (1973), 657–78.

407 LEVINE, Daniel. "Jane Addams: Romantic Radical, 1889–1912." *Mid-Am,* XLIV (1962), 195–210.

408 LEVINE, Daniel. *Jane Addams and the Liberal Tradition.* Madison, Wis., 1971.

409 LINN, James Weber. *Jane Addams.* See **174.**

410 LUBOVE, Roy. "Lawrence Veiller and the New York State Tenement House Commission of 1900." *Miss Val Hist Rev,* XLVII (1961), 659–77.

411 LUBOVE, Roy. *The Professional Altruist: The Emergence of Social Work as a Career, 1880–1930.* Cambridge, Mass., 1965.†

412 LUBOVE, Roy. "The Progressives and the Prostitute." *Historian,* XXIV (1962), 308–30.

413 LUBOVE, Roy. *The Progressives and the Slums: Tenement House Reform in New York City, 1890–1917.* Pittsburgh, 1962.

414 LUBOVE, Roy. *The Struggle for Social Security, 1900–1935.* Cambridge, Mass., 1968.

415 LUBOVE, Roy. "The Twentieth Century City: The Progressive as Municipal Reformer." *Mid-Am,* XLI (1959), 195–209.

416 RINGENBACH, Paul T. *Tramps and Reformers, 1873–1916: The Discovery of Unemployment in New York.* See **351.**

417 ROSS, Edward A. *Seventy Years of It.* See **204.**

418 STEELMAN, Lala C. "Mary Clare de Graffenried: The Saga of a Crusader for Social Reform." *East Carolina College Publications in History,* III (1966), 53–84.

419 TISHLER, Hace S. *Self-Reliance and Social Security, 1870–1917.* Port Washington, N.Y., 1971.

420 WADE, Louise C. *Graham Taylor.* See **223.**

421 WALD, Lillian D. *The House on Henry Street.* See **224.**

422 WALKER, Forrest A. "Compulsory Health Insurance: 'The Next Great Step in Social Legislation.' " *J Am Hist,* LVI (1969), 290–304.

423 WESSER, Robert F. "Conflict and Compromise: The Workmen's Compensation Movement in New York, 1890s–1913." *Lab Hist,* XII (1971), 345–72.

424 WOOD, Stephen B. *Constitutional Politics in the Progressive Era.* Chicago, 1967. (A study of the constitutional aspects of the campaign to establish federal child labor legislation.)

425 WOODS, Robert A., and Albert J. KENNEDY. *The Settlement Horizon: A National Estimate.* New York, 1922.

426 ZIMMERMAN, Jane. "The Penal Reform Movement in the South during the Progressive Era, 1890–1917." *J S Hist,* XVII (1951), 462–92.

D. The Social Gospel Movement

427 ABELL, Aaron I. *American Catholicism and Social Action.* Garden City, N.Y., 1960.

428 ABELL, Aaron I. *The Urban Impact on American Protestantism, 1865–1900.* Cambridge, Mass., 1943.

429 AIKEN, John R., and James R. MC DONNELL. "Walter Rauschenbusch and Labor Reform: A Social Gospeller's Approach." *Lab Hist,* XI (1970), 131–50.

430 BARKER, John Marshall. *The Social Gospel and the New Era.* New York, 1919.

431 BARNARD, John. *From Evangelicalism to Progressivism at Oberlin College, 1866–1917.* Columbus, Ohio, 1969.

432 DORN, Jacob H. *Washington Gladden: Prophet of the Social Gospel.* Columbus, Ohio, 1967.

433 HOPKINS, Charles H. *The Rise of the Social Gospel in American Protestantism, 1865–1915* New Haven, 1940.

434 MAY, Henry F. *Protestant Churches and Industrial America.* New York, 1949.

435 MILLER, Robert M. "Methodism and American Society, 1900–1939." *The History of American Methodism.* Eds. Emory Stevens Bucke, *et al.* 3 vols. New York, 1964. Vol. III, 328–406.

436 MULLER, Dorothea R. "The Social Philosophy of Josiah Strong: Social Christianity and American Progressivism." *Church Hist,* XXVIII (1959), 183–201.

437 RAUSCHENBUSCH, Walter. *Christianity and the Social Crisis.* New York, 1907.

438 RAUSCHENBUSCH, Walter. *A Theology for the Social Gospel.* New York, 1918.†

439 SAPPINGTON, Roger E. *Brethren Social Policy, 1908–1958.* Elgin, Ill., 1961.

440 SMITH, Willard H. "William Jennings Bryan and the Social Gospel." *J Am Hist,* LIII (1966), 41–60.

441 STELZLE, Charles. *American Social and Religious Conditions.* New York, 1912.

442 WHITE, Ronald C., Jr. and C. Howard HOPKINS, eds. *The Social Gospel: Religion and Reform in Changing America.* Philadelphia, 1976.†

E. The Muckrakers

443 CHAMBERS, David M. *The Social and Political Ideas of the Muckrakers.* New York, 1964.

444 CRUNDEN, Robert M. *A Hero in Spite of Himself: Brand Whitlock in Art, Politics, & War.* See **107.**

445 FILLER, Louis. *Appointment at Armageddon: Muckraking and Progressives in the American Tradition.* Westport, Conn., 1976.

446 FILLER, Louis. *The Muckrakers: Crusaders for American Liberalism.* University Park, Pa., 1976. (A revision of *Crusaders for American Liberalism.*)†

447 FILLER, Louis, ed. *Progressivism and Muckraking.* See **9.**

448 HARRIS, Leon. *Upton Sinclair: American Rebel.* See **141.**

449 JOHNSON, Warren B. "Muckraking in the Northwest: Joe Smith and Seattle Reform." *Pac Hist Rev,* XL (1971), 478–500.

450 KAPLAN, Justin. *Lincoln Steffens.* See **154.**

451 LANE, James B. *Jacob A. Riis and the American City.* Port Washington, N.Y., 1974.

452 LYON, Peter. *Success Story: The Life and Times of S. S. McClure.* New York, 1963.

453 MOTT, Frank L. *American Journalism: A History, 1690–1960.* 3rd ed. New York, 1962.

454 MOTT, Frank L. *A History of American Magazines.* 5 vols. New York, 1930–1968.

455 REGIER, Cornelius C. *The Era of the Muckrakers.* Chapel Hill, 1932.

456 SCHULTZ, Stanley K. "The Morality of Politics: The Muckrakers' Vision of Democracy." *J Am Hist,* LII (1965), 527–47.

457 SINCLAIR, Upton. *Autobiography.* New York, 1962.

458 STEFFENS, Lincoln. *The Autobiography of Lincoln Steffens.* See **212.**

459 WILSON, Harold S. McClure's Magazine *and the Muckrakers.* Princeton, 1970.

460 WINTER, Ella, and Granville HICKS, eds. *The Letters of Lincoln Steffens.* See **230.**

F. The Conservation Movement

461 BATES, J. Leonard. "Fulfilling American Democracy: The Conservation Movement, 1907 to 1921." *Miss Val Hist Rev,* XLIV (1957), 29–57.

462 BATES, J. Leonard. *The Origins of Teapot Dome: Progressives, Parties, and Petroleum, 1909–1921.* Urbana, Ill., 1963.

463 CROSS, Whitney R. "Ideas in Politics: The Conservation Policies of the Two Roosevelts." *J Hist Ideas,* XIV (1953), 421–38.

464 DARLING, Arthur B., ed. *The Public Papers of Francis G. Newlands.* 2 vols. Boston, 1932.

465 DODDS, Gordon B. "The Stream–Flow Controversy: A Conservation Turning Point." *J Am Hist,* LVI (1969), 59–69.

466 HAYS, Samuel P. *Conservation and the Gospel of Efficiency: The Progressive Conservation Movement, 1890–1920.* Cambridge, Mass., 1959.†

467 KING, Judson. *The Conservation Fight: From Theodore Roosevelt to the Tennessee Valley Authority.* Washington, D.C., 1945.

468 LOWITT, Richard. "A Neglected Aspect of the Progressive Movement: George W. Norris and Public Control of Hydro-Electric Power, 1913–1919." *Historian,* XXVII (1965), 350–65.

469 MC GEARY, M. Nelson. *Gifford Pinchot: Forester-Politician.* See **183.**

470 PEFFER, E. Louise. *The Closing of the Public Domain: Disposal and Reservation Policies, 1900–1950.* Stanford, 1951.

471 PENICK, James, Jr. *Progressive Politics and Conservation: The Ballinger-Pinchot Affair.* Chicago, 1968.

472 PINKETT, Harold T. *Gifford Pinchot.* See **196.**

473 RICHARDSON, Elmo R. *The Politics of Conservation: Crusaders and Controversies, 1897–1913.* Berkeley, 1962.

474 ROBBINS, Roy M. *Our Landed Heritage: The Public Domain, 1776–1936.* Princeton, 1942.†

475 SWAIN, Donald C. *Wilderness Defender: Horace M. Albright and Conservation.* Chicago, 1970.

G. Agrarian Movements

476 FITE, Gilbert C. "Peter Norbeck and the Defeat of the Nonpartisan League in South Dakota." *Miss Val Hist Rev,* XXXIII (1946), 217–36.

477 JAMIESON, Stuart. *Labor Unionism in American Agriculture.* Washington, D.C., 1945.

478 MORLAN, Robert L. *Political Prairie Fire: The Nonpartisan League, 1915–1922.* Minneapolis, 1955.

479 SALOUTOS, Theodore. *Farmer Movements in the South, 1865–1933.* Berkeley, 1960.

480 SALOUTOS, Theodore. "The Rise of the Nonpartisan League in North Dakota, 1915–1917." *Ag Hist,* XX (1946), 43–61.

481 SALOUTOS, Theodore. "The Southern Cotton Association, 1905–1908." *J S Hist,* XIII (1947), 492–510.

482 SALOUTOS, Theodore, and John D. HICKS. *Agricultural Discontent in the Middle West, 1900–1939.* Madison, Wis., 1951.†

483 SHANNON, Fred A. "The Status of the Midwestern Farmer in 1900." *Miss Val Hist Rev,* XXXVII (1950), 491–510.

484 SIMKINS, Francis B. *Pitchfork Ben Tillman, South Carolinian.* See **209.**

485 WOODWARD, C. Vann. *Tom Watson: Agrarian Rebel.* See **231.**

H. Intellectual Progressivism

486 AARON, Daniel. *Men of Good Hope.* New York, 1951.†

487 AUERBACH, Jerold S. "The Patrician as Libertarian: Zechariah Chafee, Jr. and Freedom of Speech." *N Eng Q,* XLII (1969), 511–31.

488 BOURKE, Paul F. "The Status of Politics 1909–1919: *The New Republic,* Randolph Bourne and Van Wyck Brooks." *J Am Stud,* VIII (1974), 171–202.

489 COMMAGER, Henry S. *The American Mind.* New Haven, 1950.†

490 CURTI, Merle E. *The Growth of American Thought.* 3rd ed. New York, 1964.

491 CYWAR, Alan. "John Dewey: Toward Domestic Reconstruction, 1915–1920." *J Hist Ideas,* XXX (1969), 385–400.

492 CYWAR, Alan. "John Dewey in World War I: Patriotism and International Progressivism." *Am Q,* XXI (1969), 578–94.

493 DORFMAN, Joseph. *The Economic Mind in American Civilization.* 5 vols. New York, 1946–1959.

494 DORFMAN, Joseph. *Thorstein Veblen and His America.* New York, 1934.

495 FORCEY, Charles. *The Crossroads of Liberalism: Croly, Weyl, Lippmann, and the Progressive Era, 1900–1925.* New York, 1961.†

496 FOX, Daniel M. *Discovery of Abundance: Simon N. Patten and the Transformation of Social Theory.* Ithaca, N.Y., 1967.

497 GABRIEL, Ralph H. *The Course of American Democratic Thought.* 2nd ed. New York, 1956.

498 GOLDMAN, Eric F. *Rendezvous with Destiny.* New York, 1953.†

499 HARTZ, Louis. *The Liberal Tradition in America.* New York, 1955.†

500 HOFSTADTER, Richard. *The Progressive Historians: Turner, Beard, Parrington.* New York, 1968.†

501 HOOK, Sidney. *John Dewey.* New York, 1939.

502 LASCH, Christopher. *The New Radicalism in America, 1889–1963.* New York, 1965.†

503 MANN, Arthur. "British Social Thought and American Reformers of the Progressive Era." *Miss Val Hist Rev,* XLII (1956), 672–92.

504 MASON, Alpheus T. *Brandeis.* See **180.**

505 NOBLE, David W. "The New Republic and the Idea of Progress, 1914–1920." *Miss Val Hist Rev,* XXXVIII (1951), 387–402.

506 PICKENS, Donald K. *Eugenics and Progressives.* Nashville, Tenn., 1968.

507 QUANDT, Jean B. *From the Small Town to the Great Community: The Social Thought of Progressive Intellectuals.* New Brunswick, N.J., 1970.

508 UROFSKY, Melvin I. *A Mind of One Piece: Brandeis and American Reform.* New York, 1971.

509 TAGER, Jack. *The Intellectual as Urban Reformer: Brand Whitlock and the Progressive Movement.* See **365.**

510 VANCE, Maurice M. *Charles Van Hise.* See **221.**

511 WHITE, Morton. *Social Thought in America.* New York, 1949.†

4. The Republican Era, 1901–1913

512 ADAMS, Graham, Jr. *Age of Industrial Violence, 1910–1915.* New York, 1966.

513 ANDERSON, Donald F. *William Howard Taft: A Conservative's Conception of the Presidency.* Ithaca, N.Y., 1973.

514 ANDERSON, Oscar E., Jr. *The Health of a Nation: Harvey W. Wiley and the Fight for Pure Food.* Chicago, 1958.

515 BAKER, John D. "The Character of the Congressional Revolution of 1910." *J Am Hist,* LX (1973), 679–91.

516 BARFIELD, Claude E. " 'Our Share of the Booty': The Democratic Party, Cannonism, and the Payne–Aldrich Tariff." *J Am Hist,* LVII (1970), 308–23.

517 BLUM, John M. *The Republican Roosevelt.* Cambridge, Mass., 1954.†

518 BRAEMAN, John. *Albert J. Beveridge.* See **90.**

519 BRAEMAN, John. "The Square Deal in Action: A Case Study in the Growth of the 'National Police Power.' " *Change and Continuity in Twentieth-Century America.* Eds. John Braeman, *et al.* Columbus, Ohio, 1964.

520 BURTON, David H. *Theodore Roosevelt.* New York, 1972.

521 BURTON, David H. *Theodore Roosevelt and His English Correspondents: A Special Relationship of Friends.* Philadelphia, 1973.†

522 BUTT, Archibald W. *Taft and Roosevelt.* See **96.**

523 CHESSMAN, G. Wallace. *Theodore Roosevelt.* See **97.**

524 CLAY, Howard B. "Daniel Augustus Tompkins: The Role of the New South Industrialist in Politics." *East Carolina College Publications in History,* III (1966), 85–118.

525 COHEN, Naomi W. *A Dual Heritage: The Public Career of Oscar Straus.* See **99.**

526 COLETTA, Paolo E. *The Presidency of William Howard Taft.* Lawrence, Kan., 1973.

527 CORNELL, Robert J. *The Anthracite Coal Strike of 1902.* Washington, D.C., 1957.

528 CROLY, Herbert D. *Marcus Alonzo Hanna.* See **105.**

529 FOWLER, Dorothy. *John Coit Spooner.* See **116.**

530 GARRATY, John A. *Right-Hand Man.* See **119.**

531 GATEWOOD, Willard B., Jr. *Theodore Roosevelt and the Art of Controversy.* Baton Rouge, 1970.

532 GATEWOOD, Willard B., Jr. "Theodore Roosevelt and the Coinage Controversy." *Am Q,* XVIII (1966), 35–51.

533 GERMAN, James C., Jr. "The Taft Administration and the Sherman Antitrust Act." *Mid-Am,* LIV (1972), 172–86.

534 GERMAN, James C., Jr. "Taft, Roosevelt, and United States Steel." *Historian,* XXXIV (1972), 598–613.

535 GWINN, William R. *Uncle Joe Cannon, Archfoe of Insurgency.* See **134.**

536 HAGEDORN, Hermann. *The Roosevelt Family of Sagamore Hill.* See **136.**

537 HARBAUGH, William H. *Power and Responsibility.* See **138.**

538 HECHLER, Kenneth W. *Insurgency: Personalities and Politics of the Taft Era.* New York, 1940.

539 HOLLINGSWORTH, J. Rogers. *The Whirligig of Politics.* See **55.**

540 HOLMES, William F. "Whitecapping: Agrarian Violence in Mississippi, 1902–1906." *J S Hist,* XXXV (1969), 165–85.

541 HOLT, James. *Congressional Insurgents and the Party System, 1909–1916.* Cambridge, Mass., 1967. (A study of the progressive faction within the Republican party.)

542 HORNIG, Edgar A. "The Religious Issue in the Taft-Bryan Duel of 1908." *Proc Am Philos Soc,* CV (1961), 530–37.

543 HOWE, M. A. De Wolfe. *George von Lengerke Meyer.* See **148.**

544 JESSUP, Philip C. *Elihu Root.* See **151.**

545 JOHNSON, Arthur M. "Antitrust Policy in Transition, 1908: Ideal and Reality." *Miss Val Hist Rev,* XLVIII (1961), 415–34.

546 JOHNSON, Carolyn W. *Winthrop Murray Crane: A Study in Republican Leadership, 1892–1920.* Northampton, Mass., 1967.

547 LA FOLLETTE, Belle C. and Fola. *Robert M. La Follette.* See **157.**

548 LAMBERT, Oscar D. *Stephen Benton Elkins.* See **159.**

549 LANE, Ann J. *The Brownsville Affair: National Crisis and Black Reaction.* Port Washington, N.Y., 1971.

550 LEOPOLD, Richard W. *Elihu Root and the Conservative Tradition.* See **164.**

551 LINK, Arthur S. "Theodore Roosevelt in His Letters." *Yale Rev,* XLIII (1954), 589–98.

552 LOWITT, Richard. "George Norris, James J. Hill, and the Railroad Rate Bill." *Neb Hist,* XL (1959), 137–46.

553 MASON, Alpheus T. *Bureaucracy Convicts Itself: The Ballinger–Pinchot Controversy of 1910.* New York, 1941.

554 MC GEARY, M. Nelson. *Gifford Pinchot: Forester-Politician.* See **183.**

555 MERRILL, Horace S., and Marion G. *The Republican Command, 1897–1913.* Lexington, Ky., 1971.

556 MEYER, Balthasar H. *A History of the Northern Securities Case.* Madison, Wis., 1906.

557 MORISON, Elting E. *Turmoil and Tradition.* See **185.**

558 MORISON, Elting E., and John M. BLUM, eds. *The Letters of Theodore Roosevelt.* See **186.**

559 MOWRY, George E. *The Era of Theodore Roosevelt, 1900–1912.* New York, 1958.†

560 MOWRY, George E. *Theodore Roosevelt and the Progressive Movement.* Madison, Wis., 1946.†

561 O'GARA, Gordon C. *Theodore Roosevelt and the Rise of the Modern Navy.* Princeton, 1943.

562 PENICK, James, Jr. *Progressive Politics and Conservation.* See **471.**

563 PINKETT, Harold T. "The Keep Commission, 1905–1909: A Rooseveltian Effort for Administrative Reform." *J Am Hist,* LII (1965), 297–312.

564 PITKIN, William A. "Issues in the Roosevelt-Taft Contest of 1912." *Mid-Am,* XXXIV (1952), 219–32.

565 PRINGLE, Henry F. *The Life and Times of William Howard Taft.* See **197.**

566 PRINGLE, Henry F. *Theodore Roosevelt.* See **198.**

567 RIPLEY, William Z. *Railroads: Rates and Regulation.* New York 1912.

568 ROOSEVELT, Theodore. *An Autobiography.* See **200.**

569 *The Works of Theodore Roosevelt.* See **201.**

570 SAGE, Leland L. *William Boyd Allison.* See **205.**

571 SCHEINBERG, Stephen J. "Theodore Roosevelt and the A. F. of L.'s Entry into Politics, 1906–1908." *Lab Hist,* III (1962), 131–48.

572 SCHEINER, Seth M. "President Theodore Roosevelt and the Negro, 1901–1908." *J Neg Hist,* XLVII (1963), 169–83.

573 SHERMAN, Richard B. *The Republican Party and Black America: From McKinley to Hoover, 1896–1933.* Charlottesville, Va., 1973.

574 SOLVICK, Stanley D. "William Howard Taft and the Payne-Aldrich Tariff." *Miss Val Hist Rev,* L (1963), 424–42.

575 STEELMAN, Joseph F. "Republican Party Politics in North Carolina, 1902: Factions, Leaders, and Issues." *East Carolina College Publications in History,* III (1966), 119–50.

576 STEPHENSON, Nathaniel W. *Nelson W. Aldrich.* See **214.**

577 THELEN, David P. *Robert M. La Follette.* See **219.**

578 THORNBROUGH, Emma Lou. "The Brownsville Episode and the Negro Vote." *Miss Val Hist Rev,* XLIV (1957), 469–93.

579 TINSLEY, James A. "Roosevelt, Foraker, and the Brownsville Affray." *J Neg Hist,* XLI (1956), 43–65.

580 VAN RIPER, Paul P. *History of the United States Civil Service.* Evanston, Ill., 1958.

581 WARNER, Robert M. "Chase S. Osborn and the Presidential Campaign of 1912." *Miss Val Hist Rev,* XLVI (1959), 19–45.

582 WIEBE, Robert H. "The Anthracite Strike of 1902: A Record of Confusion." *Miss Val Hist Rev,* XLVIII (1961), 229–51.

583 WIEBE, Robert H. "The House of Morgan and the Executive, 1905–1913." *Am Hist Rev,* LXV (1959), 49–60.

584 WILENSKY, Norman M. *Conservatives in the Progressive Era: The Taft Republicans of 1912.* Gainsville, Fla., 1965.†

585 WISEMAN, John B. "Racism in Democratic Politics, 1904–1912." *Mid-Am,* LI (1969), 38–58.

5. The Wilson Era, 1913–1920

A. General

586 BABSON, Roger W. *W. B. Wilson and the Department of Labor.* New York, 1919.

587 BAKER, Ray Stannard. *Woodrow Wilson.* See **80.**

588 BAKER, Ray Stannard, and William E. DODD, eds. *The Public Papers of Woodrow Wilson.* See **81.**

589 BELL, Herbert C. F. *Woodrow Wilson and the People.* See **84.**

590 BLUM, John M. *Joe Tumulty and the Wilson Era.* See **86.**

591 BLUM, John M. "Woodrow Wilson: A Study in Intellect." *Confluence,* V (1957), 367–76.

592 BLUM, John M. *Woodrow Wilson and the Politics of Morality.* See **87.**

593 BRAGDON, Henry W. *Woodrow Wilson.* See **91.**

594 BROESAMLE, John J. *William Gibbs McAdoo.* See **93.**

595 BURNER, David. *The Politics of Provincialism: The Democratic Party in Transition, 1918–1932.* New York, 1968.†

596 CLIFFORD, John G. *The Citizen Soldiers: The Plattsburg Training Camp Movement, 1913–1920.* Lexington, Ky., 1972.

597 CRONON, E. David, ed. *The Cabinet Diaries of Josephus Daniels.* See **106.**

598 CRONON, E. David, ed. *The Political Thought of Woodrow Wilson.* Indianapolis, 1965.

599 DANIELS, Josephus. *The Wilson Era.* See **110.**

600 DAVIDSON, John Wells, ed. *A Crossroads of Freedom: The 1912 Campaign Speeches of Woodrow Wilson.* New Haven, 1956.

601 DE JOUVENEL, Bertrand. "Woodrow Wilson." *Confluence,* V (1957), 320–31.

602 DIAMOND, William. *The Economic Thought of Woodrow Wilson.* Baltimore, 1943.

603 DIMOCK, Marshall E. "Woodrow Wilson as Legislative Leader." *J Pol,* XIX (1957), 3–19.

604 FAUSOLD, Martin L. *James W. Wadsworth, Jr.* See **114.**

605 FERRELL, Robert H. "Woodrow Wilson: Man and Statesman." *Rev Pol,* XVIII (1956), 131–45.

606 FREIDEL, Frank. *Franklin D. Roosevelt.* See **117.**

607 GARRATY, John A. *Henry Cabot Lodge.* See **118.**

608 GARRATY, John A. *Woodrow Wilson.* See **120.**

609 GARRATY, John A. "Woodrow Wilson: A Study in Personality." See **121.**

610 GEORGE, Alexander L., and Juliette L. GEORGE. *Woodrow Wilson and Colonel House.* See **123.**

611 GRAYSON, Cary T. *Woodrow Wilson.* See **131.**

612 GREENLEE, Howard S. "The Republican Party in Division and Reunion, 1913–1920." Doctoral dissertation, University of Chicago, 1950.

613 HECKSCHER, August. "Wilson—Style in Leadership." *Confluence,* V (1957), 332–40.

614 HECKSCHER, August, ed. *The Politics of Woodrow Wilson.* New York, 1956.

615 HOLT, James. *Congressional Insurgents and the Party System, 1909–1916.* See **541.**

616 HOUSTON, David F. *Eight Years with Wilson's Cabinet, 1913 to 1920.* See **146.**

617 HUTCHINSON, William T. *Lowden of Illinois.* See **149.**

618 KERNEY, James. *The Political Education of Woodrow Wilson.* See **155.**

619 LA FOLLETTE, Belle C. and Fola. *Robert M. La Follette.* See **157.**

620 LANE, Anne W., and Louise H. WALL, eds. *The Letters of Franklin K. Lane, Personal and Political.* See **160.**

621 LATHAM, Earl, ed. *The Philosophy and Politics of Woodrow Wilson.* Chicago, 1958.

622 LINK, Arthur S. "The Higher Realism of Woodrow Wilson." *J Presby Hist,* XLI (1963), 1–13.

623 LINK, Arthur S. *The Higher Realism of Woodrow Wilson and Other Essays.* Nashville, Tenn., 1971.

624 LINK, Arthur S., *et al.,* eds. *The Papers of Woodrow Wilson.* See **167.**

625 LINK, Arthur S. *Wilson: The Road to the White House.* See **171.**

626 LINK, Arthur S. *Woodrow Wilson: A Brief Biography.* See **173.**

627 LINK, Arthur S. "Woodrow Wilson: The American as Southerner." *J S Hist,* XXXVI (1970), 3–17.

628 LINK, Arthur S. *Woodrow Wilson and the Progressive Era.* New York, 1954.†

629 LINK, Arthur S. "Woodrow Wilson and the Study of Administration." *Proc Am Phil Soc,* CXII (1968), 431–33.

630 LOWITT, Richard. *George W. Norris.* See **175.**

631 MC ADOO, William G. *Crowded Years.* See **182.**

632 MURPHY, Paul L. *The Meaning of Freedom of Speech: First Amendment Freedoms from Wilson to FDR.* Westport, Conn., 1972.†

633 NICHOLAS, Herbert G. "Wilsonianism at Mid-Century." *Centenaire Woodrow Wilson.* Geneva, 1956.

634 PAXSON, Frederic L. *American Democracy and the World War.* 3 vols. Boston, 1936–1948.

635 ROPER, Daniel C. *Fifty Years of Public Life.* See **202.**

636 SEYMOUR, Charles. *The Intimate Papers of Colonel House.* See **208.**

637 SEYMOUR, Charles. "Woodrow Wilson in Perspective." *For Aff,* XXXIV (1956), 175–86.

638 SMITH, John S. "Organized Labor and Government in the Wilson Era, 1913–1921: Some Conclusions." *Lab Hist,* III (1962), 265–86.

639 THELEN, David P. *Robert M. La Follette.* See **219.**

640 TINDALL, George B. *The Emergence of the New South.* See **71.**

641 UROFSKY, Melvin J., and David W. LEVY. *Letters of Louis D. Brandeis.* See **220.**

642 VEYSEY, Laurence R. "The Academic Mind of Woodrow Wilson." *Miss Val Hist Rev,* XLIX (1963), 613–34.

643 WALWORTH, Arthur. *Woodrow Wilson.* See **225.**

644 WEINSTEIN, Edwin A. "Denial of Presidential Disability: A Case Study of Woodrow Wilson." *Psychiatry,* XXX (1967), 376–91.

645 WEINSTEIN, Edwin A. "Woodrow Wilson's Neurological Illness." *J Am Hist,* LVII (1970), 324–51.

B. The New Freedom

646 ABRAMS, Richard M. "Woodrow Wilson and the Southern Congressmen, 1913–1916." *J S Hist,* XXII (1956), 417–37.

647 BATES, J. Leonard. *The Origins of Teapot Dome.* See **462.**

648 BLUMENTHAL, Henry. "Woodrow Wilson and the Race Question." *J Neg Hist,* XLVIII (1963), 1–21.

649 BROESAMLE, John J. "The Struggle for Control of the Federal Reserve System, 1914–1917." *Mid-Am,* LII (1970), 280–97.

650 BURDICK, Frank. "Woodrow Wilson and the Underwood Tariff." *Mid-Am,* L (1968), 272–90.

651 BURNER, David. "The Breakup of the Wilson Coalition of 1916." *Mid-Am,* XLV (1963), 18–35.

652 CLARK, John D. *The Federal Trust Policy.* See **39.**

653 DAVIDSON, John Wells. "The Response of the South to Woodrow Wilson's New Freedom, 1912–1914." Doctoral dissertation, Yale University, 1954.

654 DAVIS, G. Cullom. "The Transformation of the Federal Trade Commission, 1914–1929." *Miss Val Hist Rev,* XLIX (1962), 437–55.

655 GLASS, Carter. *An Adventure in Constructive Finance.* Garden City, N.Y., 1927.

656 GRANTHAM, Dewey W., Jr. "Southern Congressional Leaders and the New Freedom, 1913–1917." *J S Hist,* XIII (1947), 439–59.

657 HARRIS, Seymour E. *Twenty Years of the Federal Reserve Policy.* 2 vols. Cambridge, Mass., 1933.

658 HAUGHTON, Virginia. "John W. Kern: Senate Majority Leader and Labor Legislation, 1913–1917." *Mid-Am,* LVII (1975), 184–94.

659 HOHMAN, Elmo P. "Maritime Labour in the United States: The Seamen's Act and Its Historical Background." *Int Lab Rev,* XXXVIII (1938), 190–218.

660 ISE, John. *The United States Oil Policy.* New Haven, 1926.

661 JENSEN, Billie Barnes. "Woodrow Wilson's Intervention in the Coal Strike of 1914." *Lab Hist,* XV (1974), 63–77.

662 KEMMERER, Edwin W. "Six Years of Postal Savings in the United States." *Am Econ Rev,* VII (1917), 46–90.

663 KERR, James J., IV. "German-Americans and Neutrality in the 1916 Election." *Mid-Am,* XLIII (1961), 95–105.

664 KLEBANER, Benjamin J. "Potential Competition and the American Antitrust Legislation of 1914." *Bus Hist Rev,* XXXVIII (1964), 163–85.

665 LAUGHLIN, J. Laurence. *The Federal Reserve Act: Its Origins and Problems.* New York, 1933.

666 LEARY, William M., Jr. "Woodrow Wilson, Irish Americans, and the Election of 1916." *J Am Hist,* LIV (1967), 57–72.

667 LINK, Arthur S. "The Baltimore Convention of 1912." *Am Hist Rev,* L (1945), 691–713.

668 LINK, Arthur S. "The Negro as a Factor in the Campaign of 1912." *J Neg Hist,* XXXII (1947), 81-99.

669 LINK, Arthur S. "The South and the Democratic Campaign of 1910–1912." Doctoral dissertation, University of North Carolina, 1945.

670 LINK, Arthur S. "The South and the 'New Freedom': An Interpretation." *Am Sch,* XX (1951), 314–24.

671 LINK, Arthur S. "The Underwood Presidential Movement of 1912." *J S Hist,* XI (1945), 230–45.

672 LINK, Arthur S. *Wilson: Campaigns for Progressivism and Peace, 1916–1917.* See **168.**

673 LINK, Arthur S. *Wilson: The New Freedom.* See **170.**

674 MC GOVERN, George S. "The Colorado Coal Strike, 1913–1914." Doctoral dissertation, Northwestern University, 1953.

675 MC GOVERN, George S., and Leonard F. GUTTERIDGE. *The Great Coalfield War.* Boston, 1972.

676 MURRAY, Robert K. "Public Opinion, Labor, and the Clayton Act." *Historian,* XXI (1959), 255–70.

677 PERKINS, Dexter. *Charles Evans Hughes and American Democratic Statesmanship.* See **195.**

678 PORTER, Eugene. "The Colorado Coal Strike of 1913: An Interpretation." *Historian,* XII (1949), 3–27.

679 PUSEY, Merlo J. *Charles Evans Hughes.* See **199.**

680 RATNER, Sidney. *Taxation and Democracy in America.* See **65.**

681 RUBLEE, George. "The Original Plan and Early History of the Federal Trade Commission." *Proc Acad Pol Sci,* XI (1926), 114–20.

682 SEAGER, Henry R., and Charles A. GULICK. *Trust and Corporation Problems.* See **66.**

683 SHARFMAN, I. L. *The Interstate Commerce Commission.* See **67.**

684 SMITH, Rixey, and Norman BEASLEY. *Carter Glass.* See **210.**

685 SUTTON, Walter A. "Republican Progressive Senators and Preparedness, 1915–1916." *Mid-Am,* LII (1970), 155–76.

686 TAUSSIG, Frank W. *Tariff History of the United States.* See **69.**

687 TODD, A. L. *Justice on Trial: The Case of Louis D. Brandeis.* New York, 1964.†

688 UROFSKY, Melvin I. *Big Steel and the Wilson Administration: A Study in Business-Government Relations.* Columbus, Ohio, 1969.

689 UROFSKY, Melvin I. "Wilson, Brandeis and the Trust Issue, 1912–1914." *Mid-Am,* XLIX (1967), 3–28.

690 WARBURG, Paul M. *Essays on Banking Reform in the United States.* New York, 1914.

691 WARBURG, Paul M. *The Federal Reserve System.* 2 vols. New York, 1930.

692 WEISS, Nancy J. "The Negro and the New Freedom: Fighting Wilsonian Segregation." *Pol Sci Q,* LXXXIV (1969), 61–79.

693 WILLIS, Henry P. *The Federal Reserve System.* New York, 1923.

694 WOLGEMUTH, Kathleen L. "Woodrow Wilson's Appointment Policy and the Negro." *J S Hist,* XXIV (1958), 457–71.

C. The First World War and After

695 ABRAMS, Ray H. *Preachers Present Arms: A Study of Wartime Attitudes and Activities of the Churches and the Clergy in the United States, 1914–1918.* Philadelphia, 1933.

696 ADLER, Selig. "The Congressional Election of 1918." *S Atl Q,* XXXVI (1937), 447–65.

697 ARNETT, Alex M. *Claude Kitchin and the Wilson War Policies.* Boston, 1937.

698 BAGBY, Wesley M. *The Road to Normalcy: The Presidential Campaign and Election of 1920.* Baltimore, 1962.†

699 BARBEAU, Arthur E., and Florette HENRI. *The Unknown Soldiers: Black American Troops in World War I.* Philadelphia, 1974.

700 BARUCH, Bernard M. *American Industry in the War.* New York, 1941.

701 BEAVER, Daniel R. *Newton D. Baker and the American War Effort, 1917–1919.* Lincoln, Neb., 1966.

702 BEAVER, Daniel R. "Newton D. Baker and the Genesis of the War Industries Board, 1917–1918." *J Am Hist,* LII (1965), 43–58.

703 BEST, Gary D. *The Politics of American Individualism: Herbert Hoover in Transition, 1918–1921.* Westport, Conn., 1975.

704 BEST, Gary D. "President Wilson's Second Industrial Conference, 1919–1920." *Lab Hist,* XVI (1975), 505–20.

705 BING, Alexander M. *War-time Strikes and Their Adjustment.* New York, 1921.

706 BLAKEY, George T. *Historians on the Homefront: American Propagandists for the Great War.* Lexington, Ky., 1970.

707 BLUM, John M. "Nativism, Anti-Radicalism, and the Foreign Scare, 1917–1920." *Midwest Journal,* III (1950–1951), 46–53.

708 BOGART, Ernest L. *War Costs and Their Financing.* New York, 1921.

709 BRODY, David. *Labor in Crisis: The Steel Strike of 1919.* Philadelphia, 1965.

710 BURNER, David. *The Politics of Provincialism.* See **595.**

711 CHAFEE, Zechariah, Jr. *Free Speech in the United States.* Cambridge, Mass., 1941.†

712 CHATFIELD, Charles. "World War I and the Liberal Pacifist in the United States." *Am Hist Rev,* LXXV (1970), 1920–1937.

713 Chicago Commission on Race Relations. *The Negro in Chicago: A Study of Race Relations and a Race Riot.* Chicago, 1922.

714 CLARK, John M. *The Costs of the World War to the American People.* New Haven, 1931.

715 CLARKSON, Grosvenor B. *Industrial America in the World War.* Boston, 1923.

716 COBEN, Stanley. *A. Mitchell Palmer.* See **98.**

717 COBEN, Stanley. "A Study in Nativism: The American Red Scare of 1919–1920." *Pol Sci Q,* LXXIX (1964), 52–75.

718 COFFMAN, Edward M. *The War to End All Wars: The American Military Experience in World War I.* New York, 1968.

719 COIT, Margaret L. *Mr. Baruch.* See **100.**

720 COSTRELL, Edwin. *How Maine Viewed the War, 1914–1917.* Orono, Me., 1940.

721 CRAMER, Clarence H. *Newton D. Baker.* See **103.**

722 CRIGHTON, John C. *Missouri and the World War, 1914–1917.* Columbia, Mo., 1947.

723 CROWELL, Benedict, and Robert Frost WILSON. *How America Went to War.* 6 vols. New Haven, 1921.

724 CUFF, Robert D. "Bernard Baruch: Symbol and Myth in Industrial Mobilization." *Bus Hist Rev,* XLIII (1969), 115–33.

725 CUFF, Robert D. "A 'Dollar-a-Year Man' in Government: George N. Peek and the War Industries Board." *Bus Hist Rev,* XLI (1967), 404–20.

726 CUFF, Robert D. *The War Industries Board: Business–Government Relations during World War I.* Baltimore, 1973.

727 CUFF, Robert D. "Woodrow Wilson and Business–Government Relations during World War I." *Rev Pol,* XXXI (1969), 385–407.

728 CUMMINS, Cedric C. *Indiana Public Opinion and the World War, 1914–1917.* Indianapolis, 1945.

729 CURTI, Merle E. *The Roots of American Loyalty.* New York, 1946.†

730 CYWAR, Alan. "John Dewey in World War I: Patriotism and International Progressivism." See **492.**

731 DAVIS, Allen F. "Welfare, Reform and World War I." *Am Q,* XIX (1967), 516–33.

732 DRAPER, Theodore. *The Roots of American Communism.* New York, 1957.

733 ENSLEY, Philip C. "The Interchurch World Movement and the Steel Strike of 1919." *Lab Hist,* XIII (1972), 217–30.

734 GENTHE, Charles V. *American War Narratives 1917–1918: A Study and Bibliography.* New York, 1969.

735 GILBERT, Charles. *American Financing of World War I.* Westport, Conn., 1970.

736 GODFREY, Aaron A. *Government Operation of the Railroads: Its Necessity, Success, and Consequences, 1918–1920.* Austin, Tex., 1974.

737 GOLDMAN, Eric F. "Woodrow Wilson: The Test of War." *Woodrow Wilson and the World of Today.* Ed. Arthur P. Dudden. Philadelphia, 1957.

738 GRUBER, Carol S. *Mars and Minerva: World War I and the Uses of the Higher Learning in America.* Baton Rouge, 1975.

739 HAGEDORN, Hermann. *Leonard Wood.* See **135.**

740 HALL, Tom G. "Wilson and the Food Crisis: Agricultural Price Control during World War I." *Ag Hist,* XLVII (1973), 25–46.

741 HENDRICKSON, Kenneth E., Jr. "The Pro-War Socialists, the Social Democratic League and the Ill-Fated Drive for Industrial Democracy in America, 1917–1920." *Lab Hist,* XI (1970), 304–22.

742 HIMMELBERG, Robert F. "The War Industries Board and the Antitrust Question in November 1918." *J Am Hist,* LII (1965), 59–74.

743 HINES, Walker D. *War History of American Railroads.* New Haven, 1928.

744 HOVENSTINE, E. Jay, Jr. "Lessons of World War I." *Ann Am Acad Pol Soc Sci,* CCXXXVIII (1945), 180–87.

745 HURLEY, Edward N. *The Bridge to France.* Philadelphia, 1927.

746 Interchurch World Movement of North America. *Report on the Steel Strike of 1919.* New York, 1920.

747 JAFFE, Julian F. *Crusade against Radicalism: New York during the Red Scare, 1914–1924.* Port Washington, N.Y., 1972.

748 JOHNSON, Donald D. *The Challenge to American Freedoms: World War I and the Rise of the American Civil Liberties Union.* Lexington, Ky., 1963.

749 KAPLAN, Sidney. "Social Engineers as Saviors: Effects of World War I on Some American Liberals." *J Hist Ideas,* XVII (1956), 347–69.

750 KERR, K. Austin. "Decision for Federal Control: Wilson, McAdoo, and the Railroads, 1917." *J Am Hist,* LIV (1967), 550–60.

751 KESTER, Randall B. "The War Industries Board, 1917–1918: A Study in Industrial Mobilization." *Am Pol Sci Rev,* XXXIV (1940), 655–84.

752 KEVLES, Daniel J. "Federal Legislation for Engineering Experiment Stations: The Episode of World War I." *Tech & Cul,* XII (1971), 182–89.

753 KEVLES, Daniel J. "George Ellery Hale, the First World War, and the Advancement of Science in America." *Isis,* LIX (1968), 427–37.

754 KEVLES, Daniel J. "Testing the Army's Intelligence: Psychologists and the Military in World War I." *J Am Hist,* LV (1968), 565–81.

755 KNOLES, George H. "American Intellectuals and World War I." *Pacific Northwest Quarterly,* LIX (1968), 203–15.

756 KOISTINEN, Paul A. C. "The 'Industrial–Military Complex' in Historical Perspective: World War I." *Bus Hist Rev,* XLI (1967), 378–403.

757 LASSWELL, Harold D. *Propaganda Technique in the World War.* New York, 1927.†

758 LEUCHTENBURG, William E. "The New Deal and the Analogue of War." *Change and Continuity in Twentieth-Century America.* Eds. John Braemen, *et al.* Columbus, Ohio, 1964.

759 LEVINE, Lawrence W. *Defender of the Faith.* See **166.**

760 LIVERMORE, Seward W. *Politics Is Adjourned: Woodrow Wilson and the War Congress, 1916–1918.* Middletown, Conn., 1966.†

761 LIVERMORE, Seward W. "The Section Issue in the 1918 Congressional Elections." *Miss Val Hist Rev,* XXXV (1948), 29–60.

762 LUEBKE, Frederick C. *Bonds of Loyalty: German Americans and World War I.* Dekalb, Ill., 1976.

763 MOCK, James R., and Cedric LARSON. *Words that Won the War: The Story of the Committee on Public Information, 1917–1919.* Princeton, 1939.

764 MOCK, James R., and Evangeline THURBER. *Report on Demobilization.* Norman, Okla., 1944.

765 MULLENDORF, William C. *History of the United States Food Administration, 1917–1919.* Stanford, 1941.

766 MURRAY, Robert K. "Communism and the Great Steel Strike of 1919." *Miss Val Hist Rev,* XXXVIII (1951), 445–66.

767 MURRAY, Robert K. *Red Scare: A Study in National Hysteria, 1919–1920.* Minneapolis, 1955.†

768 NASH, Gerald D. "Franklin D. Roosevelt and Labor: The World War I Origins of the Early New Deal Policy." *Lab Hist,* I (1960), 39–52.

769 NEWBY, I. A. "States' Rights and Southern Congressmen during World War I." *Phylon,* XXIV (1963), 34–50.

770 NOGGLE, Burl. *Into the Twenties: The United States from Armistice to Normalcy.* Urbana, Ill., 1972.

771 NOYES, Alexander D. *The War Period of American Finance, 1908–1925.* New York, 1926.

772 O'BRIEN, Francis W., ed. *The Hoover–Wilson Wartime Correspondence.* See **189.**

773 PALMER, Frederick. *Newton D. Baker.* See **194.**

774 PAXSON, Frederic L. *American Democracy and the World War.* See **634.**

775 PAXSON, Frederic L. "The American War Government, 1917–1918." *Am Hist Rev,* XXVI (1920), 54–76.

776 PAXSON, Frederic L. "The Great Demobilization." *Am Hist Rev,* XLIV (1939), 237–51.

777 PETERSON, Horace C. *Propaganda for War.* Norman, Okla., 1939.

778 PETERSON, Horace C., and Gilbert C. FITE. *Opponents of War, 1917–1918.* Madison, Wis., 1957.†

779 PRESTON, William, Jr. *Aliens and Dissenters: Federal Suppression of Radicals, 1903–1933.* Cambridge, Mass., 1963.

780 RUDWICK, Elliott M. *Race Riot at East St. Louis, July 2, 1917.* Carbondale, Ill., 1964.†

781 SCHEIBER, Harry N. *The Wilson Administration and Civil Liberties, 1917–1921.* Ithaca, N.Y., 1960.

782 SCHEIBER, Jane L., and Harry N. SCHEIBER. "The Wilson Administration and the Wartime Mobilization of Black Americans, 1917–1918." *Lab Hist,* X (1969), 433–58.

783 SHAPIRO, Stanley. "The Great War and Reform: Liberals and Labor, 1917–19." *Lab Hist,* XII (1971), 323–44.

784 SLOSSON, Preston W. *The Great Crusade and After, 1914–1928.* New York, 1940.†

785 SMITH, Daniel M. "Lansing and the Wilson Interregnum, 1919–1920." *Historian,* XXI (1959), 135–61.

786 SWISHER, Carl B. "The Control of War Preparations in the United States." *Am Pol Sci Rev,* XXXIV (1940), 1085–1103.

787 SWISHER, Carl B. "Civil Liberties in War Time." *Pol Sci Q,* LV (1940), 321–47.

788 TAFT, Philip. "The Federal Trials of the I.W.W." *Lab Hist,* III (1962), 57–91.

789 THOMPSON, J. A. "American Progressive Publicists and the First World War, 1914–1917." *J Am Hist,* LVIII (1971), 364–83.

790 THORBURN, Neil. "A Progressive and the First World War: Frederic C. Howe." *Mid-Am,* LI (1969), 108–18.

791 THURSTON, William N. "Management–Leadership in the United States Shipping Board, 1917–1918." *American Neptune,* XXXII (1972), 155–70.

792 TOBIN, Harold J. and Percy W. BIDWELL. *Mobilizing Civilian America.* New York, 1940.

793 TRATTNER, Walter I. "Progressivism and World War I: A Re-appraisal." *Mid-Am,* XLIV (1962), 131–45.

794 TURLINGTON, Edgar W. "The World War Period." *Neutrality, Its History, Economics and Law.* Eds. Philip C. Jessup, *et al.* New York, 1936.

795 TUTTLE, William M., Jr. *Race Riot: Chicago in the Red Summer of 1919.* New York, 1970.†

796 VIERECK, George Sylvester. *Spreading Germs of Hate.* New York, 1930.

797 WARD, Robert D. "The Origins and Activities of the National Security League, 1914–1919." *Miss Val Hist Rev,* XLVII (1960), 51–65.

798 WARTH, Robert D. "The Palmer Raids." *S Atl Q,* XLVIII (1949), 1–23.

799 WATKINS, Gordon S. *Labor Problems and the Labor Administration in the United States during the World War.* Urbana, Ill., 1920.

800 WEINBERG, Sydney. "What to Tell America: The Writers' Quarrel in the Office of War Information." *J Am Hist,* LV (1968), 73–89.

801 WEINSTEIN, Edwin A. "Denial of Presidential Disability: A Case Study of Woodrow Wilson." See **644.**

802 WEINSTEIN, Edwin A. "Woodrow Wilson's Neurological Illness." See **645.**

803 WEINSTEIN, James "Anti-War Sentiment and the Socialist Party, 1917–1918." *Pol Sci Q,* LXXIV (1959), 215–39.

804 WILLIAMS, Michael. *American Catholics in the War: National Catholic War Council, 1917–1921.* New York, 1921.

805 WILLOUGHBY, William F. *Government Organization in War Time and After.* New York, 1919.

806 WITTKE, Carl. *German–Americans and the World War.* Columbus, Ohio, 1936.

807 WRESZIN, Michael. *Oswald Garrison Villard: Pacifist at War.* Bloomington, Ind., 1965.

6. *The Supreme Court*

808 BETH, Loren P. *The Development of the American Constitution, 1877–1917.* New York, 1971.†

809 BOUDIN, Louis B. *Government by Judiciary.* 2 vols. New York, 1932.

810 CORWIN, Edward S. *Commerce Power versus States' Rights.* Princeton, 1936.

811 CORWIN, Edward S. *Court over Constitution.* Princeton, 1938.

812 CORWIN, Edward S. *The Twilight of the Supreme Court.* New Haven, 1934.

813 DUNNE, Gerald T. *Monetary Decisions of the Supreme Court.* New Brunswick, N.J., 1960.

814 FINKELSTEIN, Maurice. "From *Munn v. Illinois* to *Tyson v. Banton:* A Study in Judicial Process." *Columbia Law Review,* XXVII (1927), 769–83.

815 FRANKFURTER, Felix. *Mr. Justice Holmes and the Supreme Court.* Cambridge, Mass., 1938.

816 GARRATY, John A. "Holmes's Appointment to the U.S. Supreme Court." *N Eng Q,* XXII (1949), 291–303.

817 GOEDECKE, Robert. "Holmes, Brandeis, and Frankfurter: Differences in Pragmatic Jurisprudence." *Ethics,* LXXIV (1964), 83–96.

818 HAMILTON, Walton H. "The Path of Due Process of Law." *The Constitution Reconsidered.* Ed. Conyers Read. New York, 1938.

819 KELLER, Morton. "The Judicial System and the Law of Life Insurance, 1888–1910." *Bus Hist Rev,* XXXV (1961), 317–35.

820 KELLY, Alfred H., and Winfred A. HARBISON. *The American Constitution.* 3rd ed. New York, 1963.

821 KING, Willard L. *Melville Weston Fuller: Chief Justice of the United States, 1888–1910.* New York, 1950.

822 KLINKHAMER, Marie C. *Edward Douglas White, Chief Justice of the United States.* Washington, D.C., 1943.

823 KUTLER, Stanley I. "Labor, the Clayton Act, and the Supreme Court." *Lab Hist,* III (1962), 19–38.

824 LERNER, Max. *The Mind and Faith of Justice Holmes.* Boston, 1943.

825 MASON, Alpheus T. *Brandeis.* See **180.**

826 MOTT, Rodney L. *Due Process of Law.* Indianapolis, 1926.

827 PERKINS, Dexter. *Charles Evans Hughes and American Democratic Statesmanship.* See **195.**

828 PUSEY, Merlo J. *Charles Evans Hughes.* See **199.**

829 RAGAN, Fred D. "Justice Oliver Wendell Holmes, Jr., Zechariah Chafee, Jr., and the Clear and Present Danger Test for Free Speech: The First Year, 1919." *J Am Hist,* LVIII (1971), 24–45.

830 ROCHE, John P. "Entrepreneurial Liberty and the Fourteenth Amendment." *Lab Hist,* IV (1963), 3–31.

831 ROELOFS, Vernon W. "Justice William R. Day and Federal Regulation." *Miss Val Hist Rev,* XXXVII (1950), 39–60.

832 RUMBLE, Wilfrid E., Jr. "Legal Realism, Sociological Jurisprudence and Mr. Justice Holmes." *J Hist Ideas,* XXVI (1965), 547–66.

833 TODD, A. L. *Justice on Trial.* See **687.**

834 TWISS, Benjamin R. *Lawyers and the Constitution.* Princeton, 1942.

835 WARREN, Charles. *The Supreme Court in United States History.* 2 vols. Boston, 1926.

836 WOOD, Stephen B. *Constitutional Politics in the Progressive Era.* See **424.**

7. Socialism

837 BEDFORD, Henry F. *Socialism and the Workers in Massachusetts, 1886–1912.* Amherst, Mass., 1966.

838 BRISSENDEN, Paul F. *The I.W.W.* New York, 1919.

839 CONLIN, Joseph R. *The American Radical Press, 1880–1960.* 2 vols. Westport, Conn., 1974.

840 CONLIN, Joseph R. *Big Bill Haywood and the Radical Union Movement.* Syracuse, N.Y., 1969.

841 CONLIN, Joseph R. *Bread and Roses Too: Studies of the Wobblies.* Westport, Conn., 1969.

842 CURRIE, Harold W. "Allan L. Benson, Salesman of Socialism, 1902–1916." *Lab Hist,* XI (1970), 285–303.

843 DICK, William M. *Labor and Socialism in America: The Gompers Era.* Port Washington, N.Y., 1972.

844 DUBOFSKY, Melvyn. "Success and Failure of Socialism in New York City, 1900–1918: A Case Study." *Lab Hist,* IX (1968), 361–75.

845 DUBOFSKY, Melvyn. *We Shall Be All: A History of the Industrial Workers of the World.* Chicago, 1969.

846 EGBERT, Donald D., and Stow PERSONS, eds. *Socialism and American Life.* 2 vols. Princeton, 1952.

847 FOX, Richard W. "The Paradox of 'Progressive' Socialism: The Case of Morris Hillquit, 1901–1914." *Am Q,* XXVI (1974), 127–40.

848 GINGER, Ray. *The Bending Cross.* See **124.**

849 HANDY, Robert T. "Christianity and Socialism in America, 1900–1920." *Church Hist,* XXI (1952), 39–54.

850 HENDRICKSON, Kenneth E., Jr. "The Pro-War Socialists, the Social Democratic League and the Ill-Fated Drive for Industrial Democracy in America, 1917–1920." See **741.**

851 HILLQUIT, Morris. *History of Socialism in the United States.* New York, 1910.

852 KIPNIS, Ira A. *The American Socialist Movement, 1897–1912.* New York, 1952.†

853 LASLETT, John H. M. *Labor and the Left: A Study of Socialist and Radical Influences in the American Labor Movement, 1881–1924.* New York, 1970.

854 MILLER, Sally M. "The Socialist Party and the Negro, 1901–20." *J Neg Hist,* LVI (1971), 22–229.

855 MILLER, Sally M. "Socialist Party Decline and World War I: Bibliography and Interpretation." *Science & Society,* XXXIV (1970), 398–411.

856 MILLER, Sally M. *Victor Berger and the Promise of Constructive Socialism, 1910–1920.* Westport, Conn., 1973.

857 MOORE, R. Laurence. *European Socialists and the American Promised Land.* New York, 1970.

858 MOORE, R. Laurence. "Flawed Fraternity—American Socialist Response to the Negro, 1901–1912." *Historian,* XXXII (1969), 1–18.

859 MORGAN, H. Wayne. *Eugene V. Debs: Socialist for President.* Syracuse, N.Y., 1962.

860 MORGAN, H. Wayne. "Eugene Debs and the Socialist Campaign of 1912." *Mid-Am,* XXXIX (1957), 210–26.

861 QUINT, Howard H. *The Forging of American Socialism.* Columbia, S.C., 1953.†

862 ROSENSTONE, Robert A. *Romantic Revolutionary.* See **203.**

863 SHANNON, David A. "The Socialist Party Before the First World War: An Analysis." *Miss Val Hist Rev,* XXXVIII (1951), 279–88.

864 SHANNON, David A. *The Socialist Party of America: A History.* New York, 1955.

865 SMITH, Gibbs M. *Joe Hill.* Salt Lake City, 1969.

866 STRONG, Bryan. "Historians and American Socialism, 1900–1920." *Science & Society,* XXIV (1970), 387–97.

867 THOMPSON, Arthur W. "American Socialists and the Russian Revolution of 1905." *Freedom and Reform: Essays in Honor of Henry Steele Commager.* Eds. Harold M. Hyman and Leonard W. Levy. New York, 1967.

868 TYLER, Robert L. *Rebels of the Woods: The I.W.W. in the Pacific Northwest.* Eugene, Ore., 1967.

869 WEINSTEIN, James. "Anti-War Sentiment and the Socialist Party, 1917–1918." See **803.**

870 WEINSTEIN, James. *The Decline of Socialism in America, 1912–1925.* New York, 1967.

III. The United States and Its World Relations

1. General

871 ADLER, Selig. *The Isolationist Impulse.* New York, 1957.

872 BAILEY, Thomas A. "America's Emergence as a World Power: The Myth and the Verity." *Pac Hist Rev,* XXX (1961), 1–16.

873 BAILEY, Thomas A. *The Man in the Street: The Impact of American Public Opinion on Foreign Policy.* New York, 1948.

874 BAILEY, Thomas A. "The World Cruise of the American Battleship Fleet, 1907–1909." *Pac Hist Rev,* I (1932), 389–423.

875 BEALE, Howard K. *Theodore Roosevelt and the Rise of America to World Power.* Baltimore, 1956.†

876 BEMIS, Samuel Flagg. *A Diplomatic History of the United States.* 5th ed. New York, 1965.

877 BLAKE, Nelson M. "Ambassadors at the Court of Theodore Roosevelt." *Miss Val Hist Rev,* XLII (1955), 179–206.

878 BULLOCK, Charles T., *et al.* "The Balance of Trade of the United States." *Rev Econ Stat,* I (1919), 245–46.

879 CHALLENER, Richard D. *Admirals, Generals, and American Foreign Policy, 1898–1914.* Princeton, 1973.

880 COLETTA, Paolo E. "Secretary of State William Jennings Bryan and 'Deserving Democrats.' " *Mid-Am,* XLVIII (1966), 75–98.

881 COOPER, John M., Jr. "Progressivism and American Foreign Policy: A Reconsideration." *Mid-Am,* LI (1969), 260–77.

882 DAVIS, George T. *A Navy Second to None.* New York, 1940.

883 DE NOVO, John A. "The Enigmatic Alvey A. Adee and American Foreign Relations, 1870–1924." *Prologue,* VII (1975), 69–80.

884 DINGMAN, Roger. *Power in the Pacific: The Origins of Naval Arms Limitation, 1914–22.* Chicago, 1976.

885 DULLES, Foster Rhea. *America's Rise to World Power, 1898–1954.* New York, 1955.†

886 DUROSELLE, Jean Baptiste. *From Wilson to Roosevelt: Foreign Policy of the United States, 1913–1945.* Cambridge, Mass., 1963.

887 ELLIS, L. Ethan. *Reciprocity, 1911.* New Haven, 1939.

888 ERSHKOWITZ, Herbert. *The Attitude of Business Toward American Foreign Policy, 1900–1916.* University Park, Pa., 1967.

889 ESTHUS, Raymond A. *Theodore Roosevelt and the International Rivalries.* Waltham, Mass., 1970.

890 FILENE, Peter. "The World Peace Foundation and Progressivism, 1910–1918." *N Eng Q,* XXXVI (1963), 478–501.

891 GRAEBNER, Norman A., ed. *An Uncertain Tradition: American Secretaries of State in the Twentieth Century.* New York, 1961.†

892 GREENE, Fred. "The Military View of American National Policy, 1904–1940." *Am Hist Rev,* LXVI (1961), 354–77.

893 GRENVILLE, John A. S., and George Berkeley YOUNG. *Politics, Strategy, and American Diplomacy: Studies in Foreign Policy, 1873–1917.* New Haven, 1966.

894 HART, Robert A. *The Great White Fleet: Its Voyage Around the World, 1907–1909.* Boston, 1965.

895 HERMAN, Sondra R. *Eleven Against War: Studies in American Internationalist Thought, 1898–1921.* Stanford, 1969.†

896 HINDMAN, E. James. "The General Arbitration Treaties of William Howard Taft." *Historian,* XXXVI (1973), 52–65.

897 KAUFMAN, Burton I. *Efficiency and Expansion: Foreign Trade Organization in the Wilson Administration, 1913–1921.* Westport, Conn., 1974.

898 KAUFMAN, Burton I. "Organization for Foreign Trade Expansion in the Mississippi Valley, 1900–1920." *Bus Hist Rev,* XLVI (1972), 444–65.

899 KAUFMAN, Burton I. "The Organizational Dimension of United States Economic Foreign Policy, 1900–1920." *Bus Hist Rev,* XLVI (1972), 17–44.

900 KENNAN, George F. *American Diplomacy, 1900–1950.* Chicago, 1951.†

901 KUEHL, Warren F. *Seeking World Order: The United States and International Organization to 1920.* Nashville, Tenn., 1969.

902 LEOPOLD, Richard W. "The Emergence of America as a World Power: Some Second Thoughts." *Change and Continuity in Twentieth-Century America.* Eds. John Braeman, *et al.* Columbus, Ohio, 1964.

903 LEOPOLD, Richard W. *The Growth of American Foreign Policy.* New York, 1962.

904 LEOPOLD, Richard W. "The Mississippi Valley and American Foreign Policy, 1890–1941: An Assessment and an Appeal." *Miss Val Hist Rev,* XXXVII (1951), 625–42.

905 LEWIS, Cleona. *America's Stake in International Investments.* Washington, D.C., 1938.

906 LINK, Arthur S., Jean-Baptiste DUROSELLE, Ernst FRAENKEL, and H. G. NICHOLAS. *Wilson's Diplomacy: An International Symposium.* Cambridge, Mass., 1973.

907 LIVEZEY, William E. *Mahan on Sea Power.* Norman, Okla., 1947.

908 MINGER, Ralph E. *William Howard Taft and United States Foreign Policy: The Apprenticeship Years, 1900–1908.* Urbana, Ill., 1975.

909 OSGOOD, Robert E. *Ideals and Self-Interest in America's Foreign Relations.* Chicago, 1953.†

910 PATTERSON, Thomas G. "American Businessmen and Consular Service Reform, 1890s to 1906." *Bus Hist Rev,* XL (1966), 77–97.

911 PRATT, Julius W. *Challenge and Rejection: The United States and World Leadership, 1900–1921.* New York, 1967.

912 PRISCO, Salvatore, III. *John Barrett, Progressive Era Diplomat: A Study of a Commercial Expansionist, 1887–1920.* University, Ala., 1973.

913 SCHOLES, Walter V., and Marie V. SCHOLES. *The Foreign Policies of the Taft Administration.* Columbia, Mo., 1970.

914 SPROUT, Harold, and Margaret SPROUT. *The Rise of American Naval Power.* Princeton, 1939.

915 STUART, Graham H. *The Department of State: A History of Its Organization, Procedure, and Personnel.* New York, 1949.

916 WELLS, Samuel F., Jr. "New Perspectives on Wilsonian Diplomacy: The Secular Evangelism of American Political Economy." *Perspectives in American History,* VI (1972), 389–422.

917 WERKING, Richard H. "Selling the Foreign Service: Bureaucratic Rivalry and Foreign Trade Promotion, 1903–1912." *Pac Hist Rev,* XLV (1976), 185–208.

918 WILLIAMS, Benjamin H. *Economic Foreign Policy of the United States.* New York, 1929.

919 WILLIAMS, William A. *The Tragedy of American Diplomacy.* Cleveland, 1959.†

2. Imperialism and the War with Spain

920 AUXIER, George W. "Middle Western Newspapers and the Spanish–American War, 1895–1898." *Miss Val Hist Rev,* XXVI (1940), 523–34.

921 BAILEY, Thomas A. "Dewey and the Germans at Manila Bay." *Am Hist Rev,* XLV (1939), 58–81.

922 BEISNER, Robert L. *Twelve Against Empire: The Anti-Imperialists, 1898–1900.* New York, 1968.†

923 BERNSTEIN, Barton J., and Franklin A. LIEB. "Progressive Republican Senators and American Imperialism, 1898–1916: A Reappraisal." *Mid-Am,* L (1968), 163–205.

924 BURTON, David H. *Theodore Roosevelt: Confident Imperialist.* Philadelphia, 1968.

925 BURTON, David H. "Theodore Roosevelt's Social Darwinism and Views on Imperialism." *J Hist Ideas,* XXVI (1965), 103–18.

926 CLYMER, Kenton J. "Humanitarian Imperialism: David Prescott Barrows and the White Man's Burden in the Philippines." *Pac Hist Rev,* XLV (1976), 495–518.

927 COLETTA, Paolo E. "Bryan, McKinley, and the Treaty of Paris." *Pac Hist Rev,* XXVI (1957), 131–46.

928 COLETTA, Paolo E. "McKinley, the Peace Negotiations, and the Acquisition of the Philippines." *Pac Hist Rev,* XXX (1961), 341–50.

929 COSMAS, Graham A. *An Army for Empire: The United States Army in the Spanish–American War.* Columbia, Mo., 1971.

930 DENNETT, Tyler. *John Hay.* New York, 1933.

931 DENNIS, A. L. P. "John Hay." *The American Secretaries of State and Their Diplomacy.* Ed. Samuel Flagg Bemis. Vol. IX. New York, 1929.

932 DULLES, Foster Rhea. *The Imperial Years.* New York, 1956.†

933 EYRE, James E., Jr. "Russia and the American Acquisition of the Philippines." *Miss Val Hist Rev,* XXVIII (1942), 539–62.

934 FARRELL, John T. "Archbishop Ireland and Manifest Destiny." *Cath Hist Rev,* XXXIII (1947), 269–301.

935 FONER, Philip S. "Why the United States Went to War with Spain in 1898." *Science & Society,* XXXII (1968), 39–65.

936 FREIDEL, Frank. "Dissent in the Spanish–American War and the Philippine Insurrection." *Proceedings of the Massachusetts Historical Society,* LXXXI (1969), 167–84.

937 FREIDEL, Frank. *The Splendid Little War.* Boston, 1958.

938 GATES, John M. *Schoolbooks and Krags: The United States Army in the Philippines, 1898–1902.* Westport, Conn., 1973.

939 GATEWOOD, Willard B., Jr. "Black Americans and the Quest for Empire, 1898–1903." *J S Hist,* XXXVIII (1972), 545–66.

940 GATEWOOD, Willard B., Jr. *Black Americans and the White Man's Burden, 1898–1903.* Urbana, Ill., 1975.

941 HARBAUGH, William H. *Power and Responsibility.* See **138.**

942 HARRINGTON, Fred H. "The Anti-Imperialist Movement in the United States, 1898–1900." *Miss Val Hist Rev,* XXII (1935), 211–30.

943 HARRINGTON, Fred H. "Literary Aspects of American Anti-Imperialism, 1898–1902." *N Eng Q,* X (1937), 650–67.

944 HEALY, David. *U S Expansionism: The Imperialist Urge in the 1890s.* Madison, Wis., 1970.†

945 HITCHMAN, James H. *Leonard Wood and Cuban Independence, 1898–1902.* The Hague, 1971.

946 HOFSTADTER, Richard. "Manifest Destiny and the Philippines." *America in Crisis.* Ed. Daniel Aaron. New York, 1952.

947 KARRAKER, William A. "The American Churches and the Spanish–American War." Doctoral dissertation, University of Chicago, 1940.

948 LAFEBER, Walter. *The New Empire: An Interpretation of American Expansion, 1860–1898.* Ithaca, N.Y., 1963.†

949 LASCH, Christopher. "The Anti-Imperialists, the Philippines, and the Inequality of Man." *J S Hist,* XXIV (1958), 319–31.

950 LEUCHTENBURG, William E. "Progressivism and Imperialism: The Progressive Movement and American Foreign Policy, 1898–1916." *Miss Val Hist Rev,* XXXIX (1952), 483–504.

951 LINDERMAN, Gerald F. *The Mirror of War: American Society and the Spanish–American War.* Ann Arbor, 1974.

952 MAY, Ernest R. "American Imperialism: A Reinterpretation." *Perspectives in American History,* I (1967), 123–286.

953 MAY, Ernest R. *American Imperialism: A Speculative Essay.* New York, 1968.

954 MAY, Ernest R. *Imperial Democracy.* New York, 1961.†

955 MC CORMICK, Thomas. "Insular Imperialism and the Open Door: The China Market and the Spanish-American War." *Pac Hist Rev,* XXXII (1963), 155–70.

956 MC KEE, Delber L. "Samuel Gompers, the A. F. of L., and Imperialism, 1895–1900." *Historian,* XXI (1959), 187–99.

957 MORGAN, H. Wayne. *America's Road to Empire: The War with Spain and Overseas Expansion.* New York, 1965.

958 MORGAN, H. Wayne, ed. *Making Peace with Spain: The Diary of Whitelaw Reid.* Austin, Tex., 1965.

959 MORGAN, H. Wayne. *William McKinley and His America.* Syracuse, N.Y., 1963.

960 MORISON, Elting E., and John M. BLUM, eds. *The Letters of Theodore Roosevelt.* See **186.**

961 NEALE, R. G. *Great Britain and United States Expansion: 1898–1900.* East Lansing, Mich., 1966.

962 OLCOTT, Charles S. *The Life of William McKinley.* 2 vols. Boston, 1916.

963 PRATT, Julius W. *America's Colonial Experiment.* New York, 1950.

964 PRATT, Julius W. *Expansionists of 1898.* Baltimore, 1936.†

965 PRATT, Julius W. "The 'Large Policy' of 1898." *Miss Val Hist Rev,* XIX (1932), 219–42.

966 PULESTON, William D. *Mahan: The Life and Work of Captain Alfred Thayer Mahan, U.S.N.* New Haven, 1939.

967 QUINT, Howard H. "American Socialists and the Spanish–American War." *Am Q,* X (1958), 131–41.

968 REUTER, Frank T. *Catholic Influence on American Colonial Policies, 1898–1904.* Austin, Tex., 1967.

969 SCHIRMER, Daniel B. *Republic or Empire: American Resistance to the Philippine War.* Cambridge, Mass., 1972.

970 SEARS, Louis M. "John Sherman." *The American Secretaries of State and Their Diplomacy.* Ed. Samuel Flagg Bemis. Vol IX. New York, 1929.

971 SHIPPEE, Lester B. "Germany and the Spanish–American War." *Am Hist Rev,* XXX (1925), 754–77.

972 SHIPPEE, Lester B., and Royal B. WAY. "William Rufus Day." *The American Secretaries of State and Their Diplomacy.* Ed. Samuel Flagg Bemis. Vol. IX. New York, 1929.

973 SWANBERG, W. A. *Citizen Hearst.* See **216.**

974 SWANBERG, W. A. *Pulitzer.* See **217.**

975 TOMPKINS, E. Berkeley. "Scylla and Charybdis: The Anti-Imperialist Dilemma in the Election of 1900." *Pac Hist Rev,* XXXVI (1967), 143–62.

976 WEINBERG, Albert K. *Manifest Destiny.* Baltimore, 1935.†

977 WELCH, Richard E., Jr. "Motives and Policy Objectives of Anti-Imperialists, 1898," *Mid-Am,* LI (1969), 119–29.

978 WELCH, Richard E., Jr. "Organized Religion and the Philippine–American War, 1899–1902." *Mid-Am,* LV (1973), 184–206.

979 WESTON, Rubin F. *Racism in U.S. Imperialism: The Influence of Racial Assumptions on American Foreign Policy, 1893–1946.* Columbia, S.C., 1972.†

980 WHITTAKER, William G. "Samuel Gompers, Anti-Imperialist." *Pac Hist Rev,* XXXVIII (1969), 431–46.

981 WILKERSON, Marcus M. *Public Opinion and the Spanish–American War.* Baton Rouge, 1932.

982 WILLIAMS, William A. "Brooks Adams and American Expansion." *N Eng Q* XXV (1952), 217–32.

983 WILLIAMS, William A. *The Roots of the Modern American Empire: A Study of the Growth and Shaping of Social Consciousness in a Marketplace Society.* New York, 1969.

984 WISAN, Joseph E. *The Cuban Crises as Reflected in the New York Press, 1895–1898.* New York, 1934.

3. The United States and Latin America

985 ADLER, Selig. "Bryan and Wilsonian Caribbean Penetration." *His-Am Hist Rev,* XX (1940), 198–226.

986 AMERINGER, Charles D. "The Panama Canal Lobby of Philippe Bunau–Varilla and William Nelson Cromwell." *Am Hist Rev,* LXVIII (1963), 346–63.

987 AMERINGER, Charles D. "Philippe Bunau–Varilla: New Light on the Panama Canal Treaty." *His-Am Hist Rev,* XLVI (1966), 28–52.

988 BAKER, George. "The Wilson Administration and Cuba, 1913–1921." *Mid-Am,* XLVI (1964), 48–74.

989 BEALE, Howard K. *Theodore Roosevelt and the Rise of America to World Power.* See **875.**

990 BEMIS, Samuel Flagg. *The Latin American Policy of the United States.* New York, 1943.†

991 BERBUSSE, Edward J. *The United States in Puerto Rico, 1898–1900.* Chapel Hill, 1966.

992 CALLCOTT, Wilfrid A. *The Caribbean Policy of the United States, 1890–1920.* Baltimore, 1942.

993 CALVERT, Peter. *The Mexican Revolution 1910–1914: The Diplomacy of Anglo–American Conflict.* Cambridge, Eng., 1968.

994 CLENDENEN, Clarence C. *The United States and Pancho Villa.* Ithaca, N.Y., 1961.

995 CLINE, Howard F. *The United States and Mexico.* Rev. ed. Cambridge, Mass., 1963.†

996 COLETTA, Paolo E. "William Jennings Bryan and the United States–Colombia Impasse, 1903–1921." *His-Am Hist Rev,* XLVII (1967), 486–501.

997 CUMBERLAND, Charles C. *The Mexican Revolution: Genesis Under Madero.* Austin, Tex., 1952.

998 DENNIS, A. L. P. *Adventures in American Diplomacy, 1896–1906.* New York, 1928.

999 FABELA, Isidro. *Historia Diplomática de la Revolución Mexicana.* 2 vols. Mexico City, 1958–1959.

1000 FITZGIBBON, Russell H. *Cuba and the United States, 1900–1935.* Menasha, Wis., 1935.

1001 [FULLER, Joseph V.] "William Jennings Bryan." *The American Secretaries of State and Their Diplomacy.* Ed. Samuel Flagg Bemis. Vol. X. New York, 1929.

1002 GILLETTE, Howard, Jr. "The Military Occupation of Cuba, 1899–1902: Workshop for American Progressivism." *Am Q,* XXV (1973), 410–25.

1003 GRIEB, Kenneth J. *The United States and Huerta.* Lincoln, Neb., 1969.

1004 HAGEDORN, Hermann. *Leonard Wood.* See **135.**

1005 HALEY, P. Edward. *Revolution and Intervention: The Diplomacy of Taft and Wilson with Mexico, 1910–1917.* Cambridge, Mass., 1970.

1006 HARBAUGH, William H. *Power and Responsibility.* See **138.**

1007 HEALY, David F. *Gunboat Diplomacy in the Wilson Era: The U.S. Navy in Haiti, 1915–1916.* Madison Wis., 1976.

1008 HEALY, David F. *The United States in Cuba, 1898–1902.* Madison, Wis., 1963.

1009 HILL, Larry D. *Emissaries to a Revolution: Woodrow Wilson's Executive Agents in Mexico.* Baton Rouge, 1973.

1010 HOLBO, Paul S. "Perilous Obscurity: Public Diplomacy and the Press in the Venezuelan Crisis, 1902–1903." *Historian,* XXXII (1970), 428–48.

1011 JESSUP, Philip. *Elihu Root.* See **151.**

1012 KAHLE, Louis G. "Robert Lansing and the Recognition of Venustiana Carranza." *His-Am Hist Rev,* XXXVIII (1958), 353–72.

1013 KAUFMAN, Burton I. "United States Trade and Latin America: The Wilson Years." *J Am Hist,* LVIII (1971), 342–63.

1014 LEOPOLD, Richard W. *Elihu Root and the Conservative Tradition.* See **164.**

1015 LINK, Arthur S. *Wilson: Campaigns for Progressivism and Peace, 1916–1917.* See **168.**

1016 LINK, Arthur S. *Wilson: Confusions and Crises, 1915–1916.* See **169.**

1017 LINK, Arthur S. *Wilson: The New Freedom.* See **170.**

1018 LINK, Arthur S. *Wilson: The Struggle for Neutrality, 1914–1915.* See **172.**

1019 LINK, Arthur S. *Woodrow Wilson and the Progressive Era.* See **628.**

1020 LIVERMORE, Seward W. "Battleship Diplomacy in South America: 1905–1925." *J Mod Hist,* XVI (1944), 31–48.

1021 LIVERMORE, Seward W. "Theodore Roosevelt, the American Navy, and the Venezuelan Crisis of 1902–1903." *Am Hist Rev,* LI (1946), 452–71.

1022 LOCKMILLER, David A. *Magoon in Cuba: A History of the Second Intervention, 1906–1909.* Chapel Hill, 1938.

1023 MC GANN, Thomas F. *Argentina, the United States, and the Inter-American System, 1880–1914.* Cambridge, Mass., 1957.

1024 MILLETT, Allan R. *The Politics of Intervention: The Military Occupation of Cuba, 1906–1909.* Columbus, Ohio, 1968.

1025 MINGER, Ralph E. "William H. Taft and the United States Intervention in Cuba in 1906." *His-Am Hist Rev,* XLI (1961), 75–89.

1026 MORISON, Elting E., and John M. BLUM, eds. *The Letters of Theodore Roosevelt.* See **186.**

1027 MUNRO, Dana G. "Dollar Diplomacy in Nicaragua, 1909–1913." *His-Am Hist Rev,* XXXVIII (1958), 209–34.

1028 MUNRO, Dana G. *The Five Republics of Central America.* New York, 1918.

1029 MUNRO, Dana G. *Intervention and Dollar Diplomacy in the Caribbean, 1900–1921.* Princeton, 1964.

1030 PERKINS, Dexter. *A History of the Monroe Doctrine.* Rev. ed. Boston, 1955.†

1031 PIKE, Frederick B. *Chile and the United States, 1880–1962.* Notre Dame, Ind., 1963.

1032 PRATT, Julius W. "Robert Lansing." *The American Secretaries of State and Their Diplomacy.* Ed. Samuel Flagg Bemis. Vol. X. New York, 1929.

1033 PRINGLE, Henry F. *The Life and Times of William Howard Taft.* See **197.**

1034 PRINGLE, Henry F. *Theodore Roosevelt.* See **198.**

1035 QUIRK, Robert E. *An Affair of Honor: Woodrow Wilson and the Occupation of Veracruz.* Lexington, Ky., 1962.†

1036 QUIRK, Robert E. *The Mexican Revolution, 1914–1915: The Convention of Aguascalientes.* Bloomington, Ind., 1960.

1037 RIPPY, J. Fred. "Antecedents of the Roosevelt Corollary of the Monroe Doctrine." *Pac Hist Rev,* IX (1940), 267–79.

1038 RIPPY, J. Fred. *The Capitalists and Colombia.* New York, 1931.

1039 ROOSEVELT, Theodore. *An Autobiography.* See **200.**

1040 SCHMIDT, Hans. *The United States Occupation of Haiti, 1915–1934.* New Brunswick, N.J., 1971.

1041 SCHOLES, Walter V., and Marie V. "Wilson, Grey, and Huerta." *Pac Hist Rev,* XXXVII (1968), 151–58.

1042 SCOTT, James B. "Elihu Root." *The American Secretaries of State and Their Diplomacy.* Ed. Samuel Flagg Bemis. Vol. IX. New York, 1929.

1043 SPECTOR, Ronald. "Roosevelt, the Navy, and the Venezuela Controversy: 1902–1903." *American Neptune,* XXXII (1972), 257–63.

1044 STEPHENSON, George M. *John Lind of Minnesota.* Minneapolis, 1935.

1045 TANSILL, Charles C. *The Purchase of the Danish West Indies.* Baltimore, 1932.

1046 TROW, Clifford W. "Woodrow Wilson and the Mexican Interventionist Movement of 1919." *J Am Hist,* LVIII (1971), 46–72.

1047 TULCHIN, Joseph S. *The Aftermath of War: World War I and U.S. Policy Toward Latin America.* New York, 1971.

1048 TURLINGTON, Edgar. *Mexico and Her Foreign Creditors.* New York, 1930.

1049 WELLES, Sumner. *Naboth's Vineyard: The Dominican Republic, 1844–1924.* New York, 1928.

1050 WRIGHT, Herbert F. "Philander C. Knox." *The American Secretaries of State and Their Diplomacy.* Ed. Samuel Flagg Bemis. Vol. IX. New York, 1929.

4. The United States and Europe

1051 ALLEN, H. C. *Great Britain and the United States.* London, 1955.

1052 ANDERSON, Eugene N. *The First Moroccan Crisis, 1904–1906.* Chicago, 1930.

1053 BEALE, Howard K. *Theodore Roosevelt and the Rise of America to World Power.* See **875.**

1054 BURTON, David H. "Theodore Roosevelt and Egyptian Nationalism." *Mid-Am,* XLI (1959), 88–103.

1055 BURTON, David H. "Theodore Roosevelt and his English Correspondents: The Intellectual Roots of the Anglo–American Alliance." *Mid-Am,* LIII (1971), 12–34.

1056 CAMPBELL, Alexander E. *Great Britain and the United States, 1895–1903.* London, 1960.

1057 CAMPBELL, Charles S., Jr. *Anglo-American Understanding, 1898–1903.* Baltimore, 1957.

1058 CAMPBELL, John P. "Taft, Roosevelt, and the Arbitration Treaties of 1911." *J Am Hist,* LIII (1966), 279–98.

1059 COHEN, Naomi W. "Ambassador Straus in Turkey, 1909–1910: A Note on Dollar Diplomacy." *Miss Val Hist Rev,* XLV (1959), 252–75.

1060 COKER, William S. "The Panama Canal Tolls Controversy: A Different Perspective." *J Am Hist,* LV (1968), 555–64.

1061 DANIEL, Robert L. "The Armenian Question and American–Turkish Relations, 1914–1927." *Miss Val Hist Rev,* XLVI (1959), 252–75.

1062 DAVIS, Calvin D. *The United States and the First Hague Peace Conference.* Ithaca, N.Y., 1962.

1063 DAVIS, Calvin D. *The United States and the Second Hague Peace Conference.* Durham, N.C., 1976.

1064 DENNETT, Tyler. *John Hay.* See **930.**

1065 DENNIS, A. L. P. "John Hay." See **931.**

1066 GELBER, Lionel M. *The Rise of Anglo–American Friendship: A Study in World Politics, 1898–1906.* London, 1936.

1067 GWYNN, Stephen, ed. *The Letters and Friendships of Sir Cecil Spring-Rice.* 2 vols. Boston, 1929.

1068 HALL, Luella J. "A Partnership in Peacemaking: Theodore Roosevelt and Wilhelm II." *Pac Hist Rev,* XIII (1944), 390–411.

1069 HARBAUGH, William H. *Power and Responsibility.* See **138.**

1070 HEINDEL, Richard H. *The American Impact on Great Britain, 1898–1914.* Philadelphia, 1940.

1071 JAMISON, Alden. "The Irish Question and American Diplomacy, 1895–1921." Doctoral dissertation, Harvard University, 1942.

1072 JESSUP, Philip. *Elihu Root.* See **151.**

1073 LEOPOLD, Richard W. *Elihu Root and the Conservative Tradition.* See **164.**

1074 MEIER, Heinz K. *Friendship Under Stress: U.S.–Swiss Relations, 1900–1950.* Bern, 1970.

1075 NEVINS, Allan. *Henry White: Thirty Years of American Diplomacy.* New York, 1930.

1076 PERKINS, Bradford. *The Great Rapprochement: England and the United States, 1895–1914.* New York, 1968.

1077 PRINGLE, Henry F. *The Life and Times of William Howard Taft.* See **197.**

1078 PRINGLE, Henry F. *Theodore Roosevelt.* See **198.**

1079 ROOSEVELT, Theodore. *An Autobiography.* See **200.**

1080 ROTHSTEIN, Morton. "America in the International Rivalry for the British Wheat Market, 1860–1914." *Miss Val Hist Rev,* XLVII (1960), 401–18.

1081 SCHIEBER, Clara E. *The Transformation of American Sentiment toward Germany, 1870–1914.* Boston, 1923.

1082 SCOTT, James B. "Elihu Root." See **1042.**

1083 SCOTT, James B. *The Hague Conferences of 1899 and 1907.* Baltimore, 1909.

1084 THORSON, Winston B. "American Public Opinion and the Portsmouth Peace Conference." *Am Hist Rev,* LIII (1948), 439–64.

1085 VAGTS, Alfred. *Deutschland und die Vereinigten Staaten in der Weltpolitik.* 2 vols. New York, 1935.

1086 VAGTS, Alfred. "Hopes and Fears of an American–German War, 1870–1915." *Pol Sci Q,* LIV (1939), 514–35; LV (1940), 53–76.

1087 WARD, Alan J. *Ireland and Anglo–American Relations, 1899–1921.* Toronto, 1969.

1088 WRIGHT, Herbert F. "Philander C. Knox." See **1050.**

5. The United States and Asia

1089 BAILEY, Thomas A. "California, Japan, and the Alien Land Legislation of 1913." *Pac Hist Rev,* I (1932), 36–59.

1090 BAILEY, Thomas A. "Japan's Protest Against the Annexation of Hawaii." *J Mod Hist,* III (1931), 46–61.

1091 BAILEY, Thomas A. "The Root–Takahira Agreement of 1908." *Pac Hist Rev,* IX (1940), 19–36.

1092 BAILEY, Thomas A. *Theodore Roosevelt and the Japanese–American Crises.* Stanford, 1934.

1093 BEALE, Howard K. *Theodore Roosevelt and the Rise of America to World Power.* See **875.**

1094 BEERS, Burton F. "Robert Lansing's Proposed Bargain with Japan." *Pac Hist Rev,* XXVI (1947), 319–400.

1095 BEERS, Burton F. *Vain Endeavor: Robert Lansing's Attempts to End the American–Japanese Rivalry.* Durham, N.C., 1962.

1096 BRAISTED, William R. "The Philippine Naval Base Problem, 1898–1909." *Miss Val Hist Rev,* XLI (1954), 21–40.

1097 BRAISTED, William R. *The United States Navy in the Pacific, 1898–1907.* Austin, Tex., 1958.

1098 BRAISTED, William R. *The United States Navy in the Pacific, 1909–1922.* Austin, Tex., 1971.

1099 BRAISTED, William R. "The United States Navy's Dilemma in the Pacific, 1906–1909." *Pac Hist Rev,* XXVI (1957), 235–44.

1100 BUELL, Raymond L. "The Development of Anti-Japanese Agitation in the United States." *Pol Sci Q,* XXXVII (1922), 605–38; XXXVIII (1923), 57–81.

1101 CAMERON, Meribeth E. "American Recognition Policy toward the Republic of China, 1912–1913." *Pac Hist Rev,* II (1933), 214–30.

1102 CHAY, Jongsuk. "The Taft–Katsura Memorandum Reconsidered." *Pac Hist Rev,* XXXVII (1968), 321–26.

1103 CLINARD, Outten J. *Japan's Influence on American Naval Power, 1897–1917.* Berkeley, 1947.

1104 COLETTA, Paola E. " 'The Most Thankless Task': Bryan and the California Alien Land Legislation." *Pac Hist Rev*, XXXVI (1967), 163–88.

1105 CROLY, Herbert. *Willard Straight*. New York, 1925.

1106 CURRY, Roy W. *Woodrow Wilson and Far Eastern Policy, 1913–1921*. New York, 1957.

1107 CURRY, Roy W. "Woodrow Wilson and Philippine Policy." *Miss Val Hist Rev*, XLI (1954), 435–52.

1108 DANIELS, Roger. *The Politics of Prejudice: The Anti-Japanese Movement in California and the Struggle for Japanese Exclusion*. Berkeley, 1962.†

1109 DENNETT, Tyler. *John Hay*. See **930**.

1110 DENNETT, Tyler. *Roosevelt and the Russo–Japanese War*. Garden City, N.Y., 1925.

1111 DENNIS, A. L. P. "John Hay." See **931**.

1112 ESTHUS, Raymond A. "The Changing Concept of the Open Door, 1899–1910." *Miss Val Hist Rev*, XLVI (1959), 435–54.

1113 ESTHUS, Raymond A. "The Taft–Katsura Agreement—Reality or Myth?" *J Mod Hist*, XXXI (1959), 46–51.

1114 ESTHUS, Raymond A. *Theodore Roosevelt and Japan*. Seattle, 1966.

1115 FIFIELD, Russell H. *Woodrow Wilson and the Far East: The Diplomacy of the Shantung Question*. New York, 1952.

1116 [FULLER, Joseph V.] "William Jennings Bryan." See **1001**.

1117 GRISWOLD, A. Whitney. *The Far Eastern Policy of the United States*. New Haven, 1938.

1118 GRUNDER, Garel A., and William E. LIVEZEY. *The Philippines and the United States*. Norman, Okla., 1951.

1119 HARBAUGH, William H. *Power and Responsibility*. See **138**.

1120 HARRINGTON, Fred H. *God, Mammon, and the Japanese: Dr. Horace N. Allen and Korean–American Relations, 1884–1905*. Madison, Wis., 1946.

1121 HUNT, Michael H. *Frontier Defense and the Open Door: Manchuria in Chinese–American Relations, 1895–1911*. New Haven, 1973.

1122 HUNTINGTON-WILSON, F. M. *Memoirs of an Ex-Diplomat*. Boston, 1945.

1123 IRIYE, Akira. *Pacific Estrangement: Japanese and American Expansion, 1897–1911*. Cambridge, Mass., 1972.

1124 ISRAEL, Jerry. " 'For God, for China and for Yale'—The Open Door in Action." *Am Hist Rev*, LXXV (1970), 796–807.

1125 ISRAEL, Jerry. *Progressivism and the Open Door: America and China, 1905–1921*. Pittsburgh, 1971.

1126 JESSUP, Philip C. *Elihu Root*. See **151**.

1127 LEOPOLD, Richard W. *Elihu Root and the Conservative Tradition*. See **164**.

1128 LI, Tien-yi. *Woodrow Wilson's China Policy, 1913–1917*. Kansas City, Mo., 1952.

1129 LINK, Arthur S. *Wilson: The New Freedom*. See **170**.

1130 LIVERMORE, Seward W. "The American Navy as a Factor in World Politics, 1903–1913." *Am Hist Rev*, LXIII (1958), 863–79.

1131 MC CORMICK, Thomas J. *China Market: America's Quest for Informal Empire, 1893–1901.* Chicago, 1967.†

1132 MINGER, Ralph E. "Taft's Missions to Japan: A Study in Personal Diplomacy." *Pac Hist Rev,* XXX (1961), 279–94.

1133 MORISON, Elting E., and John M. BLUM, eds. *The Letters of Theodore Roosevelt.* See **186.**

1134 NEU, Charles E. "Theodore Roosevelt and American Involvement in the Far East, 1901–1909." *Pac Hist Rev,* XXXV (1966), 433–50.

1135 NEU, Charles E. *An Uncertain Friendship: Theodore Roosevelt and Japan, 1906–1909.* Cambridge, Mass., 1967.

1136 PRATT, Julius W. "Robert Lansing." See **1032.**

1137 PRESCOTT, Francis C. "The Lansing–Ishii Agreement." Doctoral dissertation, Yale University, 1949.

1138 PRINGLE, Henry F. *The Life and Times of William Howard Taft.* See **197.**

1139 PRINGLE, Henry F. *Theodore Roosevelt.* See **198.**

1140 PUGACH, Noel. "Making the Open Door Work: Paul S. Reinsch in China, 1913–1919." *Pac Hist Rev,* XXXVIII (1969), 157–76.

1141 REINSCH, Paul S. *An American Diplomat in China.* Garden City, N.Y., 1922.

1142 REMER, C. F. *Foreign Investments in China.* New York, 1933.

1143 ROOSEVELT, Theodore. *An Autobiography.* See **200.**

1144 SAFFORD, Jeffrey J. "Experiment in Containment: The United States Steel Embargo and Japan, 1917–1918." *Pac Hist Rev,* XXXIX (1970), 439–52.

1145 SANDMEYER, Elmer C. *The Anti-Chinese Movement in California.* Urbana, Ill., 1939.

1146 SCOTT, James B. "Elihu Root." See **1042.**

1147 STANLEY, Peter W. *A Nation in the Making: The Philippines and the United States, 1899–1921.* Cambridge, Mass., 1974.

1148 STEELMAN, Lala Carr. "Senator Augustus O. Bacon, Champion of Philippine Independence." *East Carolina College Publications in History,* II (1965), 91–113.

1149 TATE, Merze. *The United States and the Hawaiian Kingdom: A Political History.* New Haven, 1965.

1150 THORSON, Winston B. "American Public Opinion and the Portsmouth Peace Conference." See **1084.**

1151 TRANI, Eugene P. *The Treaty of Portsmouth.* Lexington, Ky., 1969.

1152 TREAT, Payson J. *Diplomatic Relations Between the United States and Japan, 1895–1905.* Stanford, 1938.

1153 TUPPER, Eleanor, and George E. MC REYNOLDS. *Japan in American Public Opinion.* New York, 1937.

1154 VARG, Paul A. *The Making of a Myth: The United States and China, 1897–1912.* East Lansing, Mich., 1968.

1155 VARG, Paul A. *Missionaries, Chinese, and Diplomats.* Princeton, 1958.

1156 VARG, Paul A. "The Myth of the China Market, 1890–1912." *Am Hist Rev,* LXXIII (1968), 742–58.

1157 VARG, Paul A. *Open Door Diplomat: The Life of W. W. Rockhill.* Urbana, Ill., 1952.

1158 VARG, Paul A. "William Woodville Rockhill and the Open Door Notes." *J Mod Hist,* XXIV (1952), 375–79.

1159 VEVIER, Charles. "The Open Door: An Idea in Action, 1906–1913." *Pac Hist Rev,* XXIV (1955), 49–62.

1160 VEVIER, Charles. *The United States and China, 1906–1913.* New Brunswick, N.J., 1955.

1161 WHITE, John A. "As the Russians Saw Our China Policy." *Pac Hist Rev,* XXVI (1957), 146–60.

1162 WHITE, John A. *The Diplomacy of the Russo–Japanese War.* Princeton, 1964.

1163 WRIGHT, Herbert F. "Philander C. Knox." See **1050.**

1164 ZABRISKIE, Edward H. *American–Russian Rivalry in the Far East, 1895–1914.* Philadelphia, 1946.

6. *The Road to War, 1914–1917*

1165 ALLEN, Howard W. "Republican Reformers and Foreign Policy, 1913–1917." *Mid-Am,* XLIV (1962), 222–29.

1166 BAILEY, Thomas A. "The Sinking of the *Lusitania.*" *Am Hist Rev,* XLI (1935), 54–73.

1167 BAILEY, Thomas A. "The United States and the Blacklist during the Great War." *J Mod Hist,* VI (1934), 14–35.

1168 BAILEY, Thomas A. "World War Analogues of the *Trent* Affair." *Am Hist Rev,* XXXVIII (1933), 286–90.

1169 BAILEY, Thomas A., and Paul B. RYAN. *The Lusitania Disaster: An Episode in Modern Warfare and Diplomacy.* New York, 1975.

1170 BAKER, Ray Stannard. *Woodrow Wilson.* See **80.**

1171 BERNSTORFF, Johann H. von. *My Three Years in America.* New York, 1920.

1172 BETHMANN HOLLWEG, Theobald von. *Betrachtungen zum Weltkriege.* 2 vols. Berlin, 1919–1922.

1173 BILLINGTON, Monroe. "The Gore Resolution of 1916." *Mid-Am,* XLVII (1965), 89–98.

1174 BIRDSALL, Paul. "Neutrality and Economic Pressures, 1914–1917." *Science and Society,* III (1939), 217–28.

1175 BIRNBAUM, Karl E. *Peace Moves and U-Boat Warfare.* Stockholm, 1958.

1176 BRYAN, Mary B., ed. *The Memoirs of William Jennings Bryan.* See **95.**

1177 BUCHANAN, Russell. "Theodore Roosevelt and American Neutrality, 1914–1917." *Am Hist Rev,* XLIII (1938), 775–90.

1178 BUEHRIG, Edward H. "Wilson's Neutrality Re-Examined." *World Politics,* III (1950) 1–19.

1179 BUEHRIG, Edward H. *Woodrow Wilson and the Balance of Power.* Bloomington, Ind., 1955.

1180 CAMBON, Henri, ed. *Paul Cambon, Correspondence, 1870–1924.* 3 vols. Paris, 1940–1946.

1181 CHILD, Clifton J. *The German–Americans in Politics, 1914–1917.* Madison, Wis., 1939.

1182 CHURCHILL, Winston S. *The World Crisis.* 6 vols. London, 1932.

1183 COOPER, John M., Jr. *The Vanity of Power: American Isolationism and the First World War, 1914–1917.* Westport, Conn., 1969.

1184 CRIGHTON, John C. "The *Wilhelmina:* An Adventure in the Assertion and Exercise of American Trading Rights during the World War." *Am J Int Law,* XXXIV (1940), 74–88.

1185 CRONON, E. David, ed. *The Cabinet Diaries of Josephus Daniels.* See **106.**

1186 CUDDY, Edward. "Pro-Germanism and American Catholicism, 1914–1917." *Cath Hist Rev,* LIV (1968), 427–54.

1187 CURTI, Merle E. *Bryan and World Peace.* Northamptom, Mass., 1931.

1188 DANIELS, Josephus. *The Wilson Era.* See **110.**

1189 DEVLIN, Patrick. *Too Proud to Fight: Woodrow Wilson's Neutrality.* New York, 1974.

1190 DOERRIES, Reinhard R. *Washington-Berlin 1908/1917: Die Tätigkeit des Botschafters Johann Heinrich Graf von Bernstorff in Washington vor dem Eintritt der Vereinigten Staaten von Amerika in den Ersten Weltkrieg.* Düsseldorf, 1975.

1191 DUBIN, Martin D. "Elihu Root and the Advocacy of a League of Nations, 1914–1917." *W Pol Q,* XIX (1966), 439–55.

1192 EPSTEIN, Klaus. *Matthias Erzberger and the Dilemma of German Democracy.* Princeton, 1959.

1193 FISCHER, Fritz. *Germany's Aims in the First World War.* New York, 1967.† (A translation of *Griff nach der Weltmach.*)

1194 FLEMING, Denna F. *The Origins and Legacies of World War I.* Garden City, N.Y., 1968.

1195 FULLER, Joseph V. "The Genesis of the Munitions Traffic." *J Mod Hist,* VI (1934), 280–93.

1196 GERARD, James W. *My Four Years in Germany.* New York, 1917.

1197 GREGORY, Ross. "A New Look at the *Dacia.*" *J Am Hist,* LV (1968), 292–96.

1198 GREGORY, Ross. *The Origins of American Intervention in the First World War.* New York, 1971.†

1199 GREGORY, Ross. *Walter Hines Page.* See **133.**

1200 GREW, Joseph C. *Turbulent Era: A Diplomatic Record of Forty Years, 1904–45.* 2 vols. Boston, 1952.

1201 GREY, Edward (Viscount Grey of Fallodon). *Twenty-Five Years, 1892–1916.* 2 vols. New York, 1925.

1202 GWYNN, Stephen, ed. *The Letters and Friendships of Sir Cecil Spring–Rice.* See **1067.**

1203 HAGEDORN, Hermann. *The Bugle That Woke America.* New York, 1940.

1204 HAGEDORN, Hermann. *Leonard Wood.* See **135.**

1205 HARBAUGH, William H. "Wilson, Roosevelt, and American Interventionism, 1914–1917." Doctoral dissertation, Northwestern University, 1954.

1206 HEINRICHS, Waldo H., Jr. *American Ambassador: Joseph C. Grew and the Development of the U.S. Diplomatic Tradition.* Boston, 1967.

1207 HENDRICK, Burton J. *The Life and Letters of Walter H. Page.* See **144.**

1208 HERRING, George C., Jr. "James Hay and the Preparedness Controversy, 1915–1916." *J S Hist,* XXX (1964), 383–404.

1209 HIRST, David W. "German Propaganda in the United States, 1914–1917." Doctoral dissertation, Northwestern University, 1962.

1210 JOHNSON, Niel M. *George Sylvester Viereck: German–American Propagandist.* Urbana, Ill., 1972.

1211 LANGER, William L. "From Isolation to Mediation." *Woodrow Wilson and the World of Today.* Ed. Arthur P. Dudden. Philadelphia, 1957.

1212 LEOPOLD, Richard W. "The Problem of American Intervention in 1917: An Historical Retrospect." *World Politics,* II (1950), 404–25.

1213 LINK, Arthur S. "The Cotton Crisis, the South, and Anglo–American Diplomacy, 1914–1915." *Studies in Southern History in Memory of Albert Ray Newsome.* Ed. J. C. Sitterson. Chapel Hill, 1957.

1214 LINK, Arthur S. *Wilson: Campaigns for Progressivism and Peace, 1916–1917.* See **168.**

1215 LINK, Arthur S. *Wilson: Confusions and Crises, 1915–1916.* See **169.**

1216 LINK, Arthur S. *Wilson the Diplomatist.* Baltimore, 1957.†

1217 LINK, Arthur S. *Wilson: The Struggle for Neutrality, 1914–1915.* See **172.**

1218 LLOYD GEORGE, David. *The War Memoirs of David Lloyd George.* 6 vols. London, 1933–1936.

1219 LOWITT, Richard. "The Armed-Ship Bill Controversy: A Legislative View." *Mid-Am,* XLVI (1964), 38–47.

1220 MAY, Ernest R. "American Policy and Japan's Entrance into World War I." *Miss Val Hist Rev,* XL (1953), 279–90.

1221 MAY, Ernest R. *The World War and American Isolation, 1914–1917.* Cambridge, Mass., 1959.†

1222 MILLIS, Walter. *Road to War: America, 1914–1917.* Boston, 1935.

1223 MOONEY, Chase C., and Martha E. LAYMAN. "Some Phases of the Compulsory Military Training Movement, 1914–1920." *Miss Val Hist Rev,* XXXVIII (1952), 633–56.

1224 MORRISSEY, Alice. *The American Defense of Neutral Rights, 1914–1917.* Cambridge, Mass., 1939.

1225 NOTTER, Harley. *The Origins of the Foreign Policy of Woodrow Wilson.* Baltimore, 1937.

1226 PALMER, Frederick. *Newton D. Baker.* See **194.**

1227 POINCARÉ, Raymond. *Au Service de la France, Neuf Années de Souvenirs.* 10 vols. Paris, 1926–1933.

1228 PRATT, Julius W. "Robert Lansing." See **1032.**

1229 RAPPAPORT, Armin. *The British Press and Wilsonian Neutrality.* Stanford, 1951.

1230 READ, James M. *Atrocity Propaganda, 1914–1919.* New Haven, 1941.

1231 RITTER, Gerhard. *Staatskunst und Kriegshandwerk.* Vol. III. Munich, 1964.

1232 RYLEY, Thomas W. *A Little Group of Willful Men: A Study of Congressional–Presidential Authority.* Port Washington, N.Y., 1975.

1233 SCHMITT, Bernadotte E. "American Neutrality, 1914–1917." *J Mod Hist,* VIII (1936), 200–11.

1234 SEYMOUR, Charles. *American Neutrality, 1914–1917.* New Haven, 1935.

1235 SEYMOUR, Charles. *The Intimate Papers of Colonel House.* See **208.**

1236 SINEY, Marion. *The Allied Blockade of Germany, 1914–1916.* Ann Arbor, Mich., 1957.

1237 SINEY, Marion. "British Negotiations with American Meat Packers, 1915–1917: A Study of Belligerent Trade Controls." *J Mod Hist,* XXIII (1951), 343–53.

1238 SMITH, Daniel M. "National Interest and American Intervention, 1917: An Historiographical Appraisal." *J Am Hist,* LIII (1965), 5–24.

1239 SMITH, Daniel M. *Robert Lansing and American Neutrality, 1914–1917.* Berkeley, 1958.

1240 SMITH, Daniel M. "Robert Lansing and the Formulation of American Neutrality Policies, 1914–1915." *Miss Val Hist Rev,* XLIII (1956), 59–81.

1241 SPINDLER, Arno. *Der Handelskrieg mit U-booten.* 3 vols. Berlin, 1932–1934.

1242 SQUIRES, James D. *British Propaganda at Home and in the United States from 1914 to 1917.* Cambridge, Mass., 1935.

1243 SUTTON, Walter A. "Progressive Republican Senators and the Submarine Crisis, 1915–1916." *Mid-Am,* XLVII (1965), 75–88.

1244 SYRETT, Harold C. "The Business Press and American Neutrality, 1914–1917." *Miss Val Hist Rev,* XXXII (1945), 215–30.

1245 TIRPITZ, Alfred von. *Politische Dokumente von A. von Tirpitz.* 2 vols. Stuttgart and Berlin, 1924–1926.

1246 VAN ALSTYNE, Richard W. "The Policy of the United States Regarding the Declaration of London, at the Outbreak of the Great War." *J Mod Hist,* VII (1935), 434–47.

1247 VAN ALSTYNE, Richard W. "Private American Loans to the Allies, 1914–1916." *Pac Hist Rev,* II (1933), 180–93.

1248 VIERECK, George Sylvester. *Spreading Germs of Hate.* See **796.**

1249 WALWORTH, Arthur. *Woodrow Wilson.* See **225.**

1250 WEINSTEIN, James. "Anti-War Sentiment and the Socialist Party." See **803.**

7. The First World War, Versailles, and the Great Betrayal

1251 ABRAHAMS, Paul P. "American Bankers and the Economic Tactics of Peace: 1919." *J Am Hist,* LVI (1969), 572–83.

THE UNITED STATES AND ITS WORLD RELATIONS

1252 AMBROSIUS, Lloyd E. "Wilson, the Republicans, and French Security after World War I." *J Am Hist,* LIX (1972), 341–52.

1253 BAILEY, Thomas A. *The Policy of the United States toward the Neutrals, 1917–1918.* Baltimore, 1942.

1254 BAILEY, Thomas A. *Woodrow Wilson and the Great Betrayal.* New York, 1945.†

1255 BAILEY, Thomas A. *Woodrow Wilson and the Lost Peace.* New York, 1944.†

1256 BAKER, Ray Stannard. *Woodrow Wilson and the World Settlement.* 3 vols. Garden City, N.Y., 1922.

1257 BARTLETT, Ruhl J. *The League to Enforce Peace.* Chapel Hill, 1944.

1258 BIRDSALL, Paul. *Versailles Twenty Years After.* New York, 1941.

1259 BUEHRIG, Edward H., ed. *Wilson's Foreign Policy in Perspective.* Bloomington, Ind., 1957.

1260 BURNETT, Philip M. *Reparations at the Paris Peace Conference from the Standpoint of the American Delegation.* 2 vols. Cambridge, Mass., 1940.

1261 CHURCHILL, Winston S. *The World Crisis.* See **1182.**

1262 COFFMAN, Edward M. *The Hilt of the Sword: The Career of Peyton C. March.* Madison, Wis., 1966.

1263 CRAMER, Clarence H. *Newton D. Baker.* See **103.**

1264 CREEL, George. *Rebel at Large.* See **104.**

1265 CRONON, E. David, ed. *The Cabinet Diaries of Josephus Daniels.* See **106.**

1266 CURRENT, Richard N. "The United States and 'Collective Security': Notes on the History of an Idea." *Isolation and Security.* Ed. Alexander DeConde. Durham, N.C., 1957.

1267 CURRY, George. "Woodrow Wilson, Jan Smuts, and the Versailles Settlement." *Am Hist Rev,* LXVI (1961), 968–86.

1268 DANIELS, Josephus. *The Wilson Era.* See **110.**

1269 Department of the Army. *The United States Army in the World War, 1917–1919.* 13 vols. Washington, D.C., 1948.

1270 DE WEERD, Harvey A. *President Wilson Fights His War: World War I and the American Intervention.* New York, 1968.

1271 DIGNAN, Don K. "The Hindu Conspiracy in Anglo–American Relations during World War I." *Pac Hist Rev,* XL (1971), 57–76.

1272 DUFF, John B. "The Versailles Treaty and the Irish–Americans." *J Am Hist,* LV (1968), 582–98.

1273 EPSTEIN, Klaus. *Matthias Erzberger and the Dilemma of German Democracy.* See **1192.**

1274 FERRELL, Robert H. "Woodrow Wilson and Open Diplomacy." *Issues and Conflicts: Studies in Twentieth Century American Diplomacy.* Ed. George L. Anderson. Lawrence, Kan., 1959.

1275 FIKE, Claude E. "The Influence of the Creel Committee and the American Red Cross on Russian–American Relations, 1917–1919." *J Mod Hist,* XXXI (1959), 93–109.

1276 FIKE, Claude E. "The United States and Russian Territorial Problems, 1917–1920." *Historian,* XXIV (1962), 331–46.

1277 FISCHER, Fritz. *Germany's Aims in the First World War.* See **1193.**

1278 FLANNAGAN, John H., Jr. "The Disillusionment of a Progressive: U.S. Senator David I. Walsh and the League of Nations Issue, 1918–1920." *N Eng Q,* XLI (1968), 483–504.

1279 FLEMING, Denna F. *The United States and the League of Nations, 1918–1920.* New York, 1932.

1280 FLOTO, Inga. *Colonel House at Paris: A Study of American Policy at the Paris Peace Conference 1919.* Aarhus, Denmark, 1973.

1281 FOSDICK, Raymond B. *Letters on the League of Nations.* Princeton, 1966.

1282 FOWLER, Wilton B. *British–American Relations 1917–1918: The Role of Sir William Wiseman.* Princeton, 1969.

1283 FREIDEL, Frank. *Over There.* Boston, 1964.

1284 FROTHINGHAM, Thomas G. *The Naval History of the World War.* 3 vols. Cambridge, Mass., 1925–1926.

1285 FRY, Michael G. *Illusions of Security: North Atlantic Diplomacy, 1918–22.* Toronto, 1972.

1286 GARRATY, John A. *Henry Cabot Lodge.* See **118.**

1287 GELFAND, Lawrence E. *The Inquiry: American Preparations for Peace, 1917– 1919.* New Haven, 1963.

1288 GERSON, Louis L. *Woodrow Wilson and the Rebirth of Poland, 1914–1920.* New Haven, 1953.

1289 GRANTHAM, Dewey W., Jr. "The Southern Senators and the League of Nations." *N Car Hist Rev,* XXVI (1949), 187–205.

1290 GRAVES, William S. *America's Siberian Adventure, 1918–1920.* New York, 1931.

1291 GREW, Joseph C. *Turbulent Era.* See **1200.**

1292 GWYNN, Stephen, ed. *The Letters and Friendships of Sir Cecil Spring–Rice.* See **1067.**

1293 HARBORD, James G. *America in the World War.* Boston, 1933.

1294 HELBICH, Wolfgang J. "American Liberals in the League of Nations Controversy." *Pub Opin Q,* XXXI (1967–1968), 568–96.

1295 HENDRICK, Burton J. *The Life and Letters of Walter H. Page.* See **144.**

1296 HEWES, James E. "Henry Cabot Lodge and the League of Nations." *Proc Am Philos Soc,* LXXXV (1970), 245–55.

1297 HOGAN, Michael J. "The United States and the Problem of International Economic Control: American Attitudes Toward European Reconstruction, 1918– 1920." *Pac Hist Rev,* XLIV (1975), 84–103.

1298 HOLT, W. Stull. *Treaties Defeated by the Senate.* Baltimore, 1933.

1299 HOOVER, Herbert. *The Ordeal of Woodrow Wilson.* New York, 1958.

1300 HUDSON, James J. *Hostile Skies: A Combat History of the American Air Service in World War I.* Syracuse, N.Y., 1968.

1301 JENSEN, Joan M. *The Price of Vigilance.* Chicago, 1968. (Civil liberties during World War I.)

1302 KENNAN, George F. *The Decision to Intervene.* Princeton, 1958.†

1303 KENNAN, George F. *Russia Leaves the War.* Princeton, 1956.

1304 KIHL, Mary R. "A Failure of Ambassadorial Diplomacy." *J Am Hist,* LVII (1970), 636–53.

1305 KLEIN, Ira. "Whitehall, Washington, and the Anglo–Japanese Alliance, 1919–1921." *Pac Hist Rev,* XLI (1972), 460–83.

1306 LANCASTER, James L. "The Protestant Churches and the Fight for Ratification of the Versailles Treaty." *Pub Opin Q,* XXXI (1967–1968), 597–619.

1307 LANGER, William L. "Peace and the New World Order." *Woodrow Wilson and the World of Today.* Ed. Arthur P. Dudden. Philadelphia, 1957.

1308 LANGER, William L. "Woodrow Wilson: His Education in World Affairs." *Confluence,* V (1956), 183–94.

1309 LANSING, Robert. *The Peace Negotiations.* Boston, 1921.

1310 LANSING, Robert. *War Memoirs of Robert Lansing.* Indianapolis, 1935.

1311 LASCH, Christopher. "American Intervention in Siberia: A Reinterpretation." *Pol Sci Q,* LXXVII (1962), 205–23.

1312 LASCH, Christopher. *The American Liberals and the Russian Revolution.* New York, 1962.

1313 LEBOW, Richard N. "Woodrow Wilson and the Balfour Declaration." *J Mod Hist,* XL (1968), 501–23.

1314 LEVIN, N. Gordon, Jr. *Woodrow Wilson and World Politics: America's Response to War and Revolution.* New York, 1968.†

1315 LINK, Arthur S. *Wilson the Diplomatist.* See **1216.**

1316 LLOYD GEORGE, David. *The War Memoirs of David Lloyd George.* See **1218.**

1317 LOGAN, Rayford W. *The Senate and the Versailles Mandate System.* Washington, D.C., 1945.

1318 LOUIS, William R. *Great Britain and Germany's Lost Colonies, 1914–1919.* London, 1967.

1319 LOWER, Richard C. "Hiram Johnson: The Making of an Irreconcilable." *Pac Hist Rev,* LXI (1972), 505–26.

1320 LOWRY, Bullitt. "Pershing and the Armistice." *J Am Hist,* LV (1968), 281–91.

1321 MAMATEY, Victor S. *The United States and East Central Europe, 1914–1919.* Princeton, 1957.

1322 MANTOUX, Paul. *Les délibérations du Conseil des quatre, 24 mars—28 juin 1919.* 2 vols. Paris, 1955. (For a translated edition, see John Boardman Witton, *Paris Peace Conference 1919* [Geneva, 1964].)

1323 MARTIN, Laurence W. *Peace Without Victory: Woodrow Wilson and the British Liberals.* New Haven, 1958.

1324 MARTIN, Laurence W. "Woodrow Wilson's Appeals to the Peoples of Europe: British Radical Influence on the President's Strategy." *Pol Sci Q,* LXXIV (1959), 498–516.

1325 MAXWELL, Kenneth R. "Irish–Americans and the Fight for Treaty Ratification." *Pub Opin Q,* XXXI (1967–1968), 620–41.

1326 MAYER, Arno J. *Political Origins of the New Diplomacy, 1917–1918.* New Haven, 1959.

1327 MAYER, Arno J. *Politics and Diplomacy of Peacemaking: Containment and Counterrevolution at Versailles, 1918–1919.* New York, 1967.

1328 MERRITT, Richard L. "Woodrow Wilson and the 'Great and Solemn Referendum,' 1920." *Rev Pol,* XXVII (1965), 78–104.

1329 MERVIN, David. "Henry Cabot Lodge and the League of Nations." *J Am Stud,* IV (1971), 201–14.

1330 MILLER, David Hunter. *My Diary at the Conference of Paris.* 21 vols. New York, 1924.

1331 MORISON, Elting E. *Admiral Sims and the Modern American Navy.* Boston, 1942.

1332 MOTT, T. Bentley. *Myron T. Herrick, Friend of France.* Garden City, N.Y., 1929.

1333 NELSON, Keith L. *Victors Divided: America and the Allies in Germany, 1918–1923.* Berkeley, 1975.

1334 NICOLSON, Harold. *Peacemaking, 1919.* Boston, 1933.†

1335 O'BRIEN, Francis W., ed. *The Hoover–Wilson Wartime Correspondence.* See **189.**

1336 O'GRADY, Joseph P., ed. *The Immigrants' Influence on Wilson's Peace Policies.* Lexington, Ky., 1967.

1337 OSGOOD, Robert E. "Woodrow Wilson, Collective Security, and the Lessons of History." *Confluence,* V (1957), 341–54.

1338 PALMER, Frederick. *Bliss, Peacemaker.* New York, 1934.

1339 PALMER, Frederick. *Newton D. Baker.* See **194.**

1340 PARRINI, Carl P. *Heir to Empire: United States Economic Diplomacy, 1916–1923.* Pittsburgh, 1969.

1341 PERKINS, Dexter. "Woodrow Wilson's Tour." *America in Crisis.* Ed. Daniel Aaron. New York, 1952.

1342 PERSHING, John J. *Final Report of General John J. Pershing.* Washington, D.C., 1919.

1343 PERSHING, John J. *My Experiences in the World War.* 2 vols. New York, 1931.

1344 POINCARÉ, Raymond. *Au Service de la France, Neuf Années de Souvenirs.* See **1227.**

1345 POSEY, John P. "David Hunter Miller and the Far Eastern Question at the Paris Peace Conference, 1919." *Southern Quarterly,* VII (1969), 373–92.

1346 PRATT, Julius W. "Robert Lansing." See **1032.**

1347 PRUESSEN, Ronald W. "John Foster Dulles and Reparations at the Paris Peace Conference, 1919: Early Patterns of a Life." *Perspectives in American History,* VIII (1974), 381–412.

1348 RITTER, Gerhard. *Staatskunst und Krieghandwerk.* Vol. IV. Munich, 1968.

1349 RUDIN, Harry R. *Armistice, 1918.* New Haven, 1944.

1350 SCHEIBER, Harry N. "World War I as Entrepreneurial Opportunity: Willard Straight and the American International Corporation." *Pol Sc Q,* LXXXIV (1969), 486–511.

1351 SEYMOUR, Charles. *American Diplomacy during the World War.* Baltimore, 1934.

1352 SEYMOUR, Charles. *The Intimate Papers of Colonel House.* See **208.**

THE UNITED STATES AND ITS WORLD RELATIONS

1353 SIMS, William S. *The Victory at Sea.* Garden City, N.Y., 1920.

1354 SMITH, Daniel M. *Aftermath of War: Bainbridge Colby and Wilsonian Diplomacy, 1920–1921. Philadelphia, 1970.*

1355 SNELL, John L. "Benedict XV, Wilson, Michaelis, and German Socialism." *Cath Hist Rev,* XXXVII (1951), 151–78.

1356 SNELL, John L. "Wilson's Peace Program and German Socialism, January–March 1918." *Miss Val Hist Rev,* XXXVIII (1951), 187–214.

1357 SPARGO, John. "Bainbridge Colby." *The American Secretaries of State and Their Diplomacy.* Ed. Samuel Flagg Bemis. Vol. IX. New York, 1929.

1358 STARTT, James D. "Early Press Reaction to Wilson's League Proposal." *Jour Q,* XXXIX (1962), 301–08.

1359 STARTT, James D. "The Uneasy Partnership: Wilson and the Press at Paris." *Mid-Am,* LII (1970), 55–69.

1360 STARTT, James D. "Wilson's Mission to Paris: The Making of a Decision." *Historian,* XXX (1968), 599–616.

1361 STONE, Ralph A. *The Irreconcilables: The Fight Against the League of Nations.* Lexington, Ky., 1970.

1362 STONE, Ralph A. "Two Illinois Senators Among the Irreconcilables." *Miss Val Hist Rev,* L (1963), 443–63.

1363 STRAKHOVSKY, Leonid I. *American Opinion about Russia, 1917–1920.* Toronto, 1961.

1364 TEMPERLEY, H. W. V., ed. *A History of the Peace Conference of Paris.* 6 vols. London, 1920–1924.

1365 THOMPSON, John M. *Russia, Bolshevism, and the Versailles Peace.* Princeton, 1966.

1366 TILLMAN, Seth P. *Anglo–American Relations at the Paris Peace Conference of 1919.* Princeton, 1961.

1367 TRANI, Eugene P. "Woodrow Wilson and the Decision to Intervene in Russia: A Reconsideration." *J Mod Hist,* XLVIII (1976), 440–61.

1368 TRASK, David F. *The United States in the Supreme War Council.* Middletown, Conn., 1961.

1369 UNTERBERGER, Betty M. *America's Siberian Expedition, 1918–1920.* Durham, N.C., 1956.

1370 UNTERBERGER, Betty M. "President Wilson and the Decision to Send American Troops to Siberia." *Pac Hist Rev,* XXIV (1955), 63–74.

1371 WALWORTH, Arthur. *Woodrow Wilson.* See **225.**

1372 WHITEMAN, Harold B., Jr., ed. *Letters from the Paris Peace Conference.* New Haven, 1965. (The letters of Charles Seymour.)

1373 WIMER, Kurt. "Woodrow Wilson Tries Conciliation: An Effort that Failed." *Historian,* XXV (1963), 419–38.

1374 WIMER, Kurt. "Woodrow Wilson's Plan for a Vote of Confidence." *Pennsylvania History,* XXVIII (1961), 2–16.

1375 WIMER, Kurt. "Woodrow Wilson's Plans to Enter the League of Nations Through an Executive Agreement." *W Pol Q,* XI (1958), 800–12.

1376 YATES, Louis A. R. *The United States and French Security, 1917–1921.* New York, 1957.

1377 ZACHAREWICZ, Mary Misela. "The Attitude of the Catholic Press toward the League of Nations." *Rec Am Cath Hist Soc,* LXVII (1956), 3–30, 88–104; LXVIII (1957), 46–50.

1378 ŽIVOJINOVIĆ, Dragan R. *America, Italy, and the Birth of Yugoslavia (1917–1919).* New York, 1973.

1379 ŽIVOJINOVIĆ, Dragan R. "Robert Lansing's Comments on the Pontifical Peace Note of August 1, 1917." *J Am Hist,* LVI (1969), 556–71.

IV. The American People and Their Economic Institutions

1. General

1380 ALLEN, Frederick Lewis. *The Lords of Creation.* New York, 1935.†

1381 BRANDES, Stuart D. *American Welfare Capitalism, 1880–1940.* Chicago, 1976.

1382 COBEN, Stanley, and Forest G. HILL, eds. *American Economic History: Essays in Interpretation.* Philadelphia, 1966.

1383 COCHRAN, Thomas C. *The American Business System: A Historical Perspective, 1900–1950.* Cambridge, Mass., 1957.

1384 COCHRAN, Thomas C., and William MILLER. *The Age of Enterprise.* New York, 1942.†

1385 DIAMOND, Sigmund. *The Reputation of the American Businessman.* Cambridge, Mass., 1955.

1386 FAULKNER, Harold U. *The Decline of Laissez Faire, 1897–1917.* New York, 1951.

1387 FRIEDMAN, Milton, and Anna Jacobson SCHWARTZ. *A Monetary History of the United States, 1867–1960.* Princeton, 1963.†

1388 GOLDSMITH, Raymond W. *Financial Intermediaries in the American Economy since 1900.* Princeton, 1958.

1389 JOHNSON, Emory R., et al. *History of Domestic and Foreign Commerce of the United States.* 2 vols. Washington, D.C., 1915.

1390 KENDRICK, John W. *Productivity Trends in the United States.* Princeton, 1961.

1391 KING, Willford I. *The National Income and Its Purchasing Power.* New York, 1930.

1392 KING, Willford I. *The Wealth and Income of the People of the United States.* New York, 1915.

1393 MITCHELL, Wesley C., et al. *Income in the United States: Its Amount and Distribution, 1909–1919.* 2 vols. New York, 1921–1922.

1394 RAUCHER, Alan R. *Public Relations and Business, 1900–1929.* Baltimore, 1968.

1395 SOULE, George. *Prosperity Decade: From War to Depression, 1917–1929.* New York, 1947.

1396 WEINSTEIN, James. *The Corporate Ideal of the Liberal State, 1900–1918.* Boston, 1968.†

1397 WILLIAMSON, Harold F., ed. *The Growth of the American Economy.* 2nd ed. Englewood Cliffs, N.J., 1957.

2. Demographic Changes

1398 BAKER, O. E. "Rural–Urban Migration and the National Welfare." *Ann Assn Am Geog,* XXIII (1933), 59–126.

1399 CHUDACOFF, Howard P. *Mobile Americans: Residential and Social Mobility in Omaha, 1880–1920.* New York, 1972.

1400 CLARK, Earle. "Contributions to Urban Growth." *Pub Am Stat Assn,* XIV (1915), 654–70.

1401 GALPIN, Charles J., and Theodore B. MANNY. *Interstate Migration among the Native White Population....* Washington, D.C., 1934.

1402 GILLETTE, John M., and George R. DAVIES. "Measure of Rural Migration and Other Factors of Urban Increase in the United States." *Pub Am Stat Assn,* XIV (1915), 642–53.

1403 GINI, Corrado, *et al. Population.* Chicago, 1930.

1404 GOODRICH, Carter, *et al. Migration and Economic Opportunity.* Philadelphia, 1936.

1405 HENRI, Florette. *Black Migration: Movement North, 1900–1920.* Garden City, N.Y., 1975.

1406 HIGGS, Robert. "The Boll Weevil, the Cotton Economy, and Black Migration, 1910–1930.' *Ag Hist,* L (1976), 335–50.

1407 HOOVER, Edgar M., Jr. "Interstate Redistribution of Population, 1850–1940." *J Econ Hist,* I (1941), 199–205.

1408 JEROME, Harry. *Migration and Business Cycles.* New York, 1926.

1409 KENNEDY, Louise V. *The Negro Peasant Turns Cityward.* New York, 1930.

1410 ROSSITER, William S. *Increase of Population in the United States, 1910–1920.* Washington, D.C., 1922.

1411 THOMPSON, Warren S., and P. K. WHELPTON. *Population Trends in the United States.* New York, 1933.

1412 THORNTHWAITE, C. Warren. *Internal Migration in the United States.* Philadelphia, 1934.

1413 WILLCOX, Walter F. *Studies in American Demography.* Ithaca, N.Y., 1940.

3. Concentration, Competition, and Public Policy

1414 BERLE, Adolf A., and Gardiner C. MEANS. *The Modern Corporation and Private Property.* New York, 1934.†

1415 BLACKFORD, Mansel G. *The Politics of Business in California 1890–1920.* Columbus, Ohio, 1976.

1416 BLAISDELL, Thomas C., Jr. *The Federal Trade Commission.* See **35.**

1417 BONBRIGHT, James C., and Gardiner C. MEANS. *The Holding Company.* New York, 1932.

1418 BUNTING, David, and Jeffery BARBOUR. "Interlocking Directorates in Large American Corporations, 1896–1964." *Bus Hist Rev,* XLV (1971), 317–35.

1419 BURNS, Arthur R. *The Decline of Competition.* New York, 1936.

1420 BURNS, Arthur R. "The Process of Industrial Concentration." *Q J Econ,* XLVII (1933), 277–311.

1421 CLARK, John Bates, and John Maurice CLARK. *The Control of Trusts.* See **38.**

1422 CLARK, John D. *The Federal Trust Policy.* See **39.**

1423 CUSHMAN, Robert E. "Social and Economic Controls through Federal Taxation." See **40.**

1424 DEWING, Arthur S. *Corporate Promotions and Reorganizations.* Cambridge, Mass., 1914.

1425 DOEZEMA, William R. "Railroad Management and the Interplay of Federal and State Regulation, 1885–1916." *Bus Hist Rev,* L (1976), 153–78.

1426 DURRAND, Edward D. *The Trust Problem.* Cambridge, Mass., 1915.

1427 EDDY, Arthur J. *The New Competition.* New York, 1912.

1428 EICHNER, Alfred S. *The Emergence of Oligopoly: Sugar Refining as a Case Study.* Baltimore, 1969.

1429 FAINSOD, Merle, and Lincoln GORDON. *Government and the American Economy.* See **42.**

1430 GALAMBOS, Louis. "The Agrarian Image of the Large Corporation, 1879–1920: A Study in Social Accommodation." *J Econ Hist,* XXVIII (1968), 341–62.

1431 GASKILL, Nelson B. *The Regulation of Competition.* New York, 1936.

1432 GERMAN, James C., Jr. "The Taft Administration and the Sherman Antitrust Act." See **533.**

1433 HAMILTON, Walton H. *Antitrust in Action.* Washington, D.C., 1940.

1434 HENDERSON, Gerard C. *The Federal Trade Commission.* New Haven, 1925.

1435 HIMMELBERG, Robert F. "Business, Antitrust Policy, and the Industrial Board of the Department of Commerce, 1919." *Bus Hist Rev,* XLII (1968), 1–23.

1436 HOOGENBOOM, Ari, and Olive HOOGENBOOM. *A History of the ICC: From Panacea to Palliative.* New York, 1976.†

1437 JENKS, Jeremiah Whipple, and Walter E. CLARK. *The Trust Problem.* 5th ed. New York, 1929.

1438 JOHNSON, Arthur M. "Antitrust Policy in Transition, 1908: Ideal and Reality." See **545**.

1439 JONES, Eliot. *The Trust Problem in the United States.* New York, 1923.

1440 KIRSH, Benjamin S. *Trade Associations, the Legal Aspects.* New York, 1928.

1441 KLEBANER, Benjamin J. "Potential Competition and the Antitrust Legislation of 1914." See **664**.

1442 KNAUTH, Oswald Whitman. *The Policy of the United States toward Industrial Monopoly.* New York, 1914.

1443 LIVESAY, Harold C., and Patrick G. PORTER. "Vertical Integration in American Manufacturing, 1899–1948." *J Econ Hist,* XXIX (1969), 494–500.

1444 MEAD, Edward Sherwood. *Trust Finance.* New York, 1914.

1445 MEYER, Balthasar Henry. *A History of the Northern Securities Case.* See **556**.

1446 MILLS, Frederick C. *Economic Tendencies in the United States.* See **62**.

1447 MITCHELL, Wesley C. *Business Cycles and Their Causes.* See **63**.

1448 MOODY, John. *The Truth about the Trusts.* New York, 1904.

1449 MOULTON, Harold G., et al. *Capital Expansion, Employment, and Economic Stability.* Washington, D.C., 1940.

1450 National Industrial Conference Board. *Trade Associations: Their Economic Significance and Legal Status.* New York, 1925.

1451 NEAL, Larry. "Trust Companies and Financial Innovation, 1897–1914." *Bus Hist Rev,* XLV (1971), 35–51.

1452 NELSON, Milton Nels. *Open Price Associations.* Urbana, Ill., 1922.

1453 RATNER, Sidney. *Taxation and Democracy in America.* See **65**.

1454 SCHLUTER, William C. *The Pre-War Business Cycle, 1907–1914.* New York, 1923.

1455 SEAGER, Henry R., and Charles A. GULICK, Jr. *Trust and Corporation Problems.* See **66**.

1456 SHARFMAN, I. L. "The Trade Association Movement." *Am Econ Rev, Supp,* XVI (1926).

1457 STEVENS, William H. S. *Unfair Competition.* Chicago, 1917.

1458 THORELLI, Hans B. *The Federal Antitrust Policy.* See **70**.

1459 UROFSKY, Melvin I. "Josephus Daniels and the Armor Trust." *N Car Hist Rev,* XLV (1968), 237–63.

1460 WATKINS, Myron W. *Industrial Combinations and Public Policy.* See **72**.

1461 WILCOX, Clair. *Competition and Monopoly in American Industry.* Washington, D.C., 1940.

4. Finance Capitalism

1462 ALLEN, Frederick Lewis. *The Great Pierpont Morgan.* New York, 1949.

1463 ALLEN, Frederick Lewis. *The Lords of Creation.* See **1380**.

1464 BRANDEIS, Louis D. *Other People's Money, and How the Bankers Use It.* New York, 1914.

1465 BROESAMLE, John J. "The Struggle for Control of the Federal Reserve System, 1914–1917." See **649.**

1466 CAROSSO, Vincent. *Investment Banking in America: A History.* Cambridge, Mass., 1970.

1467 CLEWS, Henry. *Fifty Years in Wall Street.* New York, 1908.

1468 COREY, Lewis. *The House of Morgan.* New York, 1930.

1469 DEWING, Arthur S. *The Financial Policy of Corporations.* Rev. ed. New York, 1934.

1470 DOWING, Cedric B. *Populists, Plungers, and Progressives: A Social History of Stock and Commodity Speculation, 1890–1936.* Princeton, 1965.

1471 EDWARDS, George W. *The Evolution of Finance Capitalism.* London, 1938.

1472 GARRATY, John A. *Right-Hand Man.* See **119.**

1473 GLASS, Carter. *An Adventure in Constructive Finance.* See **655.**

1474 GOODHART, C. A. E. *The New York Market and the Finance of Trade, 1900–1913.* Cambridge, Mass., 1969.

1475 HARRIS, Seymour E. *Twenty Years of Federal Reserve Policy.* See **657.**

1476 KUZNETZ, Simon. *Capital in the American Economy.* Princeton, 1961.

1477 LAUGHLIN, J. Laurence. *The Federal Reserve Act.* See **665.**

1478 MOODY, John. *Masters of Capital.* New Haven, 1921.

1479 MYERS, Margaret G., *et al. The New York Money Market.* 4 vols. New York, 1913–1932.

1480 NOYES, Alexander D. *Forty Years of American Finance, 1865–1907.* New York, 1909.

1481 NOYES, Alexander D. *The War Period of American Finance, 1908–1925.* See **771.**

1482 SEAGER, Henry R. and Charles A. GULICK. *Trust and Corporation Problems.* See **66.**

1483 SPRAGUE, O. M. W. *History of Crises under the National Banking System.* Washington, D.C., 1910.

1484 SYLLA, Richard. "Federal Policy, Banking Market Structure, and Capital Mobilization in the United States, 1863–1913." *J Econ Hist,* XXIV (1969), 657–86.

1485 WARBURG, Paul M. *The Federal Reserve System.* See **691.**

1486 WILLIS, Henry Parker. *The Federal Reserve System.* See **693.**

5. Manufacturing and Other Industries

1487 AITKEN, Hugh G. T. *Taylorism at Watertown Arsenal: Scientific Management in Action, 1908–1915.* Cambridge, Mass., 1960.

1488 ANDREANO, Ralph. "The Structure of the California Petroleum Industry, 1895–1911." *Pac Hist Rev,* XXXIX (1970), 171–92.

1489 ANDREWS, John B. *Phosphorus Poisoning in the Match Industry in the United States.* Washington, D.C., 1910.

1490 BARITZ, Loren. *The Servants of Power: A History of the Use of Social Science in American Industry.* Middletown, Conn., 1960.

1491 BERGER, Harold, and Sam H. SCHURR. *The Mining Industry: A Study of Output, Employment, and Production.* New York, 1944.

1492 BERGLUND, Abraham and Philip G. WRIGHT. *The Tariff on Iron and Steel.* Washington, D.C., 1929.

1493 BULEY, R. Carlyle. *The Equitable Life Assurance Society of the United States.* New York, 1959.

1494 CHANEY, Lucian W., and Hugh S. HANNA. *The Safety Movement in the Iron and Steel Industry in the United States.* Washington, D.C., 1918.

1495 CLARK, Victor S. *History of Manufactures.* 3 vols. New York, 1929.

1496 CLEMEN, Rudolf A. *The American Livestock and Meat Industry.* New York, 1923.

1497 COCHRAN, Thomas C. *The Pabst Brewing Company: The History of an American Business.* New York, 1948.

1498 COLE, Arthur H. *The American Wool Manufacture.* 2 vols. Cambridge, Mass., 1926.

1499 COPELAND, Melvin T. *The Cotton Manufacturing Industry of the United States.* Cambridge, Mass., 1912.

1500 COPLEY, Frank B. *Frederick W. Taylor.* 2 vols. New York, 1923.

1501 DAY, Edmund E., and Woodlief THOMAS. *The Growth of Manufactures, 1899 to 1923.* Washington, D.C., 1928.

1502 FABRICANT, Solomon. *The Output of Manufacturing Industries, 1899–1937.* New York, 1940.

1503 GARRATY, John A. *Right-Hand Man.* See **119.**

1504 GIBB, George Sweet and Evelyn H. KNOWLTON. *The Resurgent Years, 1911–1927: History of Standard Oil Company (New Jersey).* New York, 1956.

1505 HABER, Samuel. *Efficiency and Uplift.* See **255.**

1506 HAMMOND, John W. *Men and Volts: The Story of General Electric.* Philadelphia, 1941.

1507 HENDRICK, Burton J. *The Life of Andrew Carnegie.* See **143.**

1508 HESSEN, Robert. "The Transformation of Bethlehem Steel, 1904–1909." *Bus Hist Rev,* XLVI (1972), 339–60.

1509 HIDY, Ralph W., and Muriel E. HIDY. *Pioneering in Big Business, 1882–1911: History of Standard Oil Company (New Jersey).* New York, 1955.

1510 HOOVER, Edgar M., Jr. *Location Theory and the Shoe and Leather Industries.* Cambridge, Mass., 1937.

1511 ISE, John. *The United States Oil Policy.* See **660.**

1512 JAMES, Marquis. *Alfred I. Du Pont: The Family Rebel.* Indianapolis, 1941.

1513 KEIR, Malcolm. *Manufacturing.* New York, 1928.

1514 KELLER, Morton. *The Life Insurance Enterprise, 1885–1910: A Study in the Limits of Corporate Power.* Cambridge, Mass., 1963.

1515 KERR, K. Austin. *American Railroad Politics, 1914–1920: Rates, Wages, and Efficiency.* Pittsburgh, 1968.

1516 KUBE, Harold D., and Ralph H. DANKOF. *Changes in Distribution of Manufacturing Wage Earners, 1899–1939.* Washington, D.C., 1942.

1517 KUHLMANN, Charles B. *The Development of the Flour–Milling Industry in the United States.* Boston, 1929.

1518 LARSON, Henrietta M., and Kenneth W. PORTER. *History of Humble Oil & Refining Company: A Study in Industrial Growth.* New York, 1959.

1519 LOOS, John L. *Oil on Stream! A History of Interstate Pipeline Company, 1909–1959.* Baton Rouge, 1959.

1520 MAY, George S. *A Most Unique Machine: The Michigan Origins of the American Automobile Industry.* Grand Rapids, Mich., 1975.

1521 MC DONALD, Forrest. *Insull.* Chicago, 1962.

1522 MC DONALD, Forrest. *Let There Be Light: The Electric Utility Industry in Wisconsin, 1881–1955.* Madison, Wis., 1957.

1523 MC LAUGHLIN, Glenn E. *Growth of American Manufacturing Areas.* Pittsburgh, 1938.

1524 MOORE, Charles W. *Timing a Century: History of the Waltham Watch Company.* Cambridge, Mass., 1945.

1525 NASH, Gerald D. *United States Oil Policy, 1890–1964: Business and Government in Twentieth-Century America.* Pittsburgh, 1968.

1526 NELSON, Daniel. *Managers and Workers: Origins of the New Factory System in the United States, 1880–1920.* Madison, Wis., 1975.

1527 NELSON, Daniel. "Scientific Management, Systematic Management, and Labor, 1880–1915." *Bus Hist Rev,* XLVIII (1974), 479–500.

1528 NEVINS, Allan. *Study in Power: John D. Rockefeller, Industrialist and Philanthropist.* 2 vols. New York, 1953.

1529 NEWCOMER, Mabel. *The Big Business Executive.* New York, 1955.

1530 O'CONNOR, Harvey. *Mellon's Millions.* New York, 1933.

1531 SEVERSON, Robert F., Jr. "The American Manufacturing Frontier, 1870–1940." *Bus Hist Rev,* XXXIV (1960), 356–72.

1532 SMALLEY, Orange A., and Frederick D. STURDIVANT. *The Credit Merchants: A History of Spiegel, Inc.* Carbondale, Ill., 1973.

1533 STEIGERWALT, Albert K. *The National Association of Manufacturers, 1895–1914: A Study in Business Leadership.* Ann Arbor, Mich., 1964.

1534 STEIGERWALT, Albert K. "The NAM and the Congressional Investigations of 1913: A Case Study in the Suppression of Evidence." *Bus Hist Rev,* XXXIV (1960), 335–44.

1535 TARBELL, Ida M. *The Life of Elbert H. Gary.* New York, 1925.

1536 THOMPSON, Clarence B., ed. *Scientific Management.* Cambridge, Mass., 1914.

1537 THOMPSON, Tracy E. *Location of Manufactures, 1899–1929.* Washington, D.C., 1933.

1538 THORP, Willard L. *The Integration of Industrial Operations.* Washington, D.C., 1924.

1539 UROFSKY, Melvin I. *Big Steel and the Wilson Administration.* See **688.**

1540 WARSHOW, Herman T., ed. *Representative Industries in the United States.* New York, 1928.

1541 WOOD, Norman J. "Industrial Relations Policies of American Management, 1900–1933." *Bus Hist Rev,* XXXIV (1960), 403–20.

6. *Transportation*

1542 AGG, Thomas R., and John E. BRINDLEY. *Highway Administration and Finance.* New York, 1927.

1543 BONBRIGHT, James C. *Railroad Capitalization.* New York, 1920.

1544 CAINE, Stanley. "Why Railroads Supported Regulation: The Case of Wisconsin, 1905–1910." See **291.**

1545 CAMPBELL, E. G. *The Reorganization of the American Railroad System, 1893–1900.* New York, 1938.

1546 DEARING, Charles L. *American Highway Policy.* Washington, D.C., 1941.

1547 DIXON, Frank H. *Railroads and Government: Their Relations in the United States, 1910–1921.* New York, 1922.

1548 DOEZEMA, William R. "Railroad Management and the Interplay of Federal and State Regulation, 1885–1916." See **1425.**

1549 DOSTER, James F. *Railroads in Alabama Politics, 1875–1914.* University, Ala., 1957.

1550 FERGUSON, Maxwell. *State Regulation of Railroads in the South.* New York, 1916.

1551 FLINK, James J. *America Adopts the Automobile, 1895–1910.* Cambridge, Mass., 1970.

1552 GUSTIN, Lawrence R. *Billy Durant: Creator of General Motors.* Grand Rapids, Mich., 1973.

1553 HARBESON, Robert W. "Railroads and Regulation, 1877–1916: Conspiracy or Public Interest?" See **50.**

1554 HOOGENBOOM, Ari, and Olive HOOGENBOOM. *A History of the ICC.* See **1436.**

1555 HUTCHINS, John G. B. *The American Maritime Industries and Public Policy, 1789–1914.* Cambridge, Mass., 1941.

1556 KEMBLE, John H. "The Transpacific Railroads, 1869–1915." *Pac Hist Rev,* XVIII (1949) 331–44.

1557 KENNAN, George. *E. H. Harriman.* 2 vols. Boston, 1922.

1558 KENNEDY, Edward D. *The Automobile Industry.* New York, 1941.

1559 KERR, K. Austin. *American Railroad Politics, 1914–1920.* See **1515.**

1560 KOLKO, Gabriel. *Railroads and Regulation.* See **57.**

1561 LOCKLIN, D. Philip. *Economics of Transportation.* Chicago, 1935.

1562 LOWITT, Richard. "George W. Norris, James J. Hill, and the Railroad Rate Bill." See **552.**

1563 MARTIN, Albro. *Enterprise Denied: Origins of the Decline of American Railroads, 1897–1917.* See **268.**

1564 MARTIN, Albro. *James J. Hill and the Opening of the Northwest.* See **179.**

1565 MASON, Edward S. *The Street Railway in Massachusetts.* Cambridge, Mass., 1932.

1566 MAY, George S. *A Most Unique Machine.* See **1520.**

1567 MILLER, Sidney L. *Railway Transportation.* Chicago, 1925.

1568 MOULTON, Harold G. *Waterways versus Railways.* Rev. ed. Boston, 1926.

1569 MOULTON, Harold G., *et al. The American Transportation Problem.* Washington, D.C., 1933.

1570 NEVINS, Allan. *Ford, the Times, the Man, the Company.* New York, 1954.

1571 PYLE, Joseph G. *The Life of James J. Hill.* 2 vols. Garden City, N.Y., 1917.

1572 RIPLEY, William Z. *Railroads: Finance & Organization.* New York, 1920.

1573 RIPLEY, William Z. *Railroads: Rates and Regulation.* New York, 1912.

1574 SCOTT, Roy V. "American Railroads and Agricultural Extension, 1900–1914: A Study in Railway Developmental Techniques." *Bus Hist Rev,* XXXIX (1965), 74–98.

1575 SELTZER, Lawrence H. *A Financial History of the American Automobile Industry.* Boston, 1928.

1576 SHARFMAN, I. L. *The American Railroad Problem.* New York, 1921.

1577 SHARFMAN, I. L. *The Interstate Commerce Commission.* See **67.**

1578 STAPLES, Henry L., and Alpheus T. MASON. *The Fall of a Railroad Empire.* See **358.**

1579 SWARD, Keith T. *The Legend of Henry Ford.* New York, 1948.

1580 WILCOX, Delos F. *Analysis of the Electric Railway Problem.* New York, 1921.

1581 WILCOX, Delos F. *Municipal Franchises.* 2 vols. Rochester, 1910.

1582 ZEIS, Paul M. *American Shipping Policy.* Princeton, 1938.

7. Agriculture

1583 BAILEY, Joseph C. *Seaman A. Knapp, Schoolmaster of American Agriculture.* New York, 1945.

1584 BAILEY, Liberty Hyde, ed. *Cyclopedea of American Agriculture.* 4 vols. New York, 1907–1909.

1585 BARGER, Harold, and Hans H. LANDSBERG. *American Agriculture, 1899–1939.* New York, 1942.

1586 BENEDICT, Murray R. *Farm Policies of the United States, 1790–1950.* New York, 1953.

1587 BOGUE, Allan G. *Money at Interest: The Farm Mortgage on the Middle Border.* Ithaca, N.Y., 1955.

1588 BURBANK, Garin. "Agrarian Radicals and Their Opponents: Political Conflict in Southern Oklahoma, 1910–1924." *J Am Hist,* LVIII (1971), 5–23.

1589 GALAMBOS, Louis. "The Agrarian Image of the Large Corporation, 1879–1920: A Study in Social Accommodation." See **1430.**

1590 GAUS, John M., and Leon O. WOLCOTT. *Public Administration and the United States Department of Agriculture.* Chicago, 1940.

1591 GOLDENWEISER, Emanuel A., and Leon E. TRUESDALE. *Farm Tenancy in the United States.* Washington, D.C., 1924.

1592 HALL, Tom G. "Wilson and the Food Crisis: Agricultural Price Control during World War I." See **740.**

1593 HARDING, T. Swann. *Two Blades of Grass: A History of Scientific Development in the U.S. Department of Agriculture.* Norman, Okla., 1947.

1594 HARGREAVES, Mary Wilma M. *Dry Farming in the Northern Great Plains, 1900–1925.* Cambridge, Mass., 1957.

1595 HIGGS, Robert. "The Boll Weevil, the Cotton Economy, and Black Migration, 1910–1930." See **1406.**

1596 JAMIESON, Stuart. *Labor Unionism in American Agriculture.* See **477.**

1597 NOURSE, Edwin G., et al. *American Agriculture and the European Market.* New York, 1924.

1598 SALOUTOS, Theodore. *Farmer Movements in the South, 1865–1933.* See **479.**

1599 SALOUTOS, Theodore, and John D. HICKS. *Agricultural Discontent in the Middle West, 1900–1939.* See **482.**

1600 SCHLEBECKER, John T. *Whereby We Thrive: A History of American Farming, 1607–1972.* Ames, Iowa, 1975.

1601 SHANNON, Fred A. "The Status of the Midwestern Farmer in 1900." See **483.**

1602 SHEPARDSON, Whitney H. *Agricultural Education in the United States.* New York, 1929.

1603 THOMPSON, Carl W. *Cost and Sources of Farm–Mortgage Loans in the United States.* Washington, D.C., 1916.

1604 TRUE, Alfred C. *A History of Agricultural Education in the United States, 1785–1925.* Washington, D.C., 1929.

1605 TRUESDALE, Leon E. *Farm Population of the United States.* Washington, D.C., 1926.

1606 TWETON, D. Jerome. "The Golden Age of Agriculture: 1897–1917." *North Dakota History,* XXXVII (1970), 41–56.

8. Research and Technology

1607 DODDS, Gordon B. "The Stream–Flow Controversy: A Conservation Turning Point." See **465.**

1608 EPSTEIN, Ralph C. "Industrial Invention: Heroic or Systematic?" *Q J Econ,* XL (1926), 232–72.

1609 FLINN, Alfred D. *Research Laboratories in Industrial Establishments of the United States.* Washington, D.C., 1920.

1610 HAMILTON, Walton H. *Patents and Free Enterprise.* Washington, D.C., 1941.

1611 HOLLEY, I. B., Jr. *Ideas and Weapons: Exploitation of the Aerial Weapon by the United States During World War I; A Study in the Relationship of Technological Advance, Military Doctrine, and the Development of Weapons.* New Haven, 1953.

1612 HUGHES, Thomas P. *Elmer Sperry: Inventor and Engineer.* Baltimore, 1971.

1613 JEROME, Harry. *Mechanization in Industry.* New York, 1934.

1614 JOSEPHSON, Matthew. *Edison.* New York, 1959.

1615 KELLY, Fred C. *The Wright Brothers.* New York, 1943.†

1616 LORWIN, Lewis L., and John M. BLAIR. *Technology in Our Economy.* Washington, D.C., 1941.

1617 LYTLE, Richard H. "The Introduction of Diesel Power in the United States, 1897–1912." *Bus Hist Rev,* XLII (1968), 115–48.

1618 MC FARLAND, Marvin W., ed. *The Papers of Wilbur and Orville Wright, Including the Chanute–Wright Letters and Other Papers of Octave Chanute.* 2 vols. New York, 1953.

1619 MORISON, Elting E. *From Know–How to Nowhere: The Development of American Technology.* New York, 1974.

1620 OLIVER, John W. *History of American Technology.* New York, 1956.

1621 ROSEBERRY, C. R. *Glenn Curtiss: Pioneer of Flight.* Garden City, N.Y., 1972.

1622 ROSENBERG, Charles E. "Science, Technology, and Economic Growth: The Case of the Agricultural Experiment Station Scientist, 1875–1914." *Ag Hist,* XLV (1971), 1–20.

1623 SILK, Leonard S. *The Research Revolution.* New York, 1960.

1624 SMITH, Richard K. *First Across! The U.S. Navy's Transatlantic Flight of 1919.* Annapolis, 1973.

9. Labor

1625 ADAMIC, Louis. *Dynamite: The Story of Class Violence in America.* New York, 1931.

1626 ADAMS, Graham, Jr. *Age of Industrial Violence, 1910–1915.* See **512.**

1627 AIKEN, John R., and James R. MC DONNELL. "Walter Rauschenbusch and Labor Reform: A Social Gospeller's Approach." See **429.**

1628 ANDERSON, H. Dewey, and Percy E. DAVIDSON. *Occupational Trends in the United States.* Stanford, 1940.

1629 BABSON, Roger W. *W. B. Wilson and the Department of Labor.* See **586.**

1630 BERMAN, Edward. *Labor and the Sherman Act.* New York, 1930.

1631 BERMAN, Edward. *Labor Disputes and the President of the United States.* New York, 1924.

1632 BEST, Gary D. "President Wilson's Second Industrial Conference, 1919–20." See **704.**

1633 BING, Alexander M. *War-Time Strikes and Their Adjustment.* See **705.**

1634 BRANDEIS, Elizabeth. "Labor Legislation." See **36.**

1635 BRISSENDEN, Paul F. *Earnings of Factory Workers, 1899–1927.* Washington, D.C., 1929.

1636 BRISSENDEN, Paul F. *The I.W.W.* See **838.**

1637 BRODY, David. *Labor in Crisis.* See **709.**

1638 BRODY, David. *Steelworkers in America: The Nonunion Era.* Cambridge, Mass., 1960.†

1639 BRYANT, Keith L., Jr. "Kate Barnard, Organized Labor, and Social Justice in Oklahoma during the Progressive Era." See **389.**

1640 BUDER, Stanley. *Pullman: An Experiment in Industrial Order and Community Planning, 1880–1930.* New York, 1967.†

1641 CHAPIN, Robert C. *The Standard of Living among Workingmen's Families in New York City.* New York, 1909.

1642 CONLIN, Joseph R. *Big Bill Haywood and the Radical Union Movement.* See **840.**

1643 CONLIN, Joseph R. *Bread and Roses Too.* See **841.**

1644 COOMBS, Whitney. *The Wages of Unskilled Labor in Manufacturing Industries in the United States, 1890–1924.* New York, 1926.

1645 CRONIN, Bernard C. *Father Yorke and the Labor Movement in San Francisco, 1900–1910.* Washington, D.C., 1943.

1646 DAVIDSON, Elizabeth H. *Child Labor Legislation in the Southern Textile States.* See **392.**

1647 DERBER, Milton. "The Idea of Industrial Democracy in America, 1898–1915." See **397.**

1648 DICK, William M. *Labor and Socialism in America.* See **843.**

1649 DOUGLAS, Paul H. *American Apprenticeship and Industrial Education.* New York, 1921.

1650 DOUGLAS, Paul H. *Real Wages in the United States, 1890–1926.* Boston, 1930.

1651 DOUGLAS, Paul H., and Aaron DIRECTOR. *The Problem of Unemployment.* New York, 1931.

1652 DUBOFSKY, Melvyn. "Organized Labor and the Immigrant in New York City, 1900–1918." *Lab Hist,* II (1961), 182–201.

1653 DUBOFSKY, Melvyn. *We Shall Be All.* See **845.**

1654 DUBOFSKY, Melvyn. *When Workers Organize.* See **296.**

1655 EASTMAN, Crystal. *Work-Accidents and the Law.* See **398.**

1656 ENSLEY, Philip C. "The Interchurch World Movement and the Steel Strike of 1919." See **733.**

1657 FABRICANT, Solomon. *Employment in Manufacturing, 1899–1939.* New York, 1942.

1658 FAULKNER, Harold U., and Mark STARR. *Labor in America.* New York, 1944.

1659 FETHERLING, Dale. *Mother Jones: The Miner's Angel: A Portrait.* Carbondale, Ill., 1974.

1660 FINK, Gary M., *et al.,* eds. *Biographical Dictionary of American Labor Leaders.* See **10.**

1661 FOERSTER, Robert F., and Else H. DIETEL. *Employee Stock Ownership in the United States.* Princeton, 1929.

1662 FONER, Philip S. *History of the Labour Movement in the United States.* 4 vols. New York, 1947–1965.

1663 FRANKFURTER, Felix and N. GREENE. *The Labor Injunction.* New York, 1930.

1664 FRENCH, Carroll E. *The Shop Committee in the United States.* Baltimore, 1923.

1665 FROST, Richard H. *The Mooney Case.* Stanford, 1968.

1666 GALAMBOS, Louis. "AFL's Concept of Big Business: A Quantitative Study of Attitudes toward the Large Corporations, 1894–1931." *J Am Hist,* LVII (1971), 847–63.

1667 GARRATY, John A. "The United States Steel Corporation versus Labor: The Early Years." *Lab Hist,* I (1960), 3–38.

1668 GLUCK, Elsie. *John Mitchell, Miner.* New York, 1929.

1669 GOMPERS, Samuel. *Seventy Years of Life and Labor.* See **127.**

1670 GREEN, Marguerite. *The National Civic Federation and the American Labor Movement, 1900–1925.* See **48.**

1671 GREGORY, Charles O. *Labor and the Law.* New York, 1946.

1672 GRUBBS, Frank L., Jr. *The Struggle for Labor Loyalty: Gompers, the A.F. of L., and the Pacifists, 1917–1920.* Durham, N.C., 1968.

1673 HANSEN, Alvin H. "Industrial Class Alignments in the United States." *Pub Am Stat Assn,* XVII (1920), 417–25.

1674 HAUGHTON, Virginia. "John W. Kern: Senate Majority Leader and Labor Legislation, 1913–1917." See **658.**

1675 HEATH, Frederick M. "Labor and the Progressive Movement in Connecticut." See **312.**

1676 HILL, Joseph A. *Women in Gainful Occupation, 1870–1920.* Washington, D.C., 1929.

1677 HOHMAN, Elmo P. "Maritime Labour in the United States: The Seamen's Act and Its Historical Background." See **659.**

1678 HOHMAN, Elmo P. "Maritime Labour in the United States: Since the Seamen's Act." *Int Lab Rev,* XXXVIII (1938), 376–403.

1679 Interchurch World Movement of North America. *Report on the Steel Strike of 1919.* see **746.**

1680 JEFFREYS–JONES, Rhodi. "Violence in American History: Pug Uglies in the Progressive Era." *Perspectives in American History,* VIII (1974), 465–583.

1681 JENSEN, Billie Barnes. "Woodrow Wilson's Intervention in the Coal Strike of 1914." See **661.**

1682 KARSON, Marc. *American Labor Unions and Politics, 1900–1918.* See **56.**

1683 KELLOGG, Paul Underwood, ed. *The Pittsburgh Survey.* See **261.**

1684 KENNEALLY, James J. "Women and Trade Unions, 1870–1920: The Quandary of the Reformer." *Lab Hist,* XIV (1973), 42–55.

1685 KLUGER, James R. *The Clifton–Morenci Strike: Labor Difficulty in Arizona, 1915–1916.* Tucson, Ariz., 1970.

1686 KUTLER, Stanley I. "Labor, the Clayton Act, and the Supreme Court." See **823.**

1687 LAHNE, Herbert J. *The Cotton Mill Worker.* New York, 1944.

1688 LANFEAR, Vincent W. *Business Fluctuations and the American Labor Movement, 1915–1922.* New York, 1924.

1689 LASLETT, John H. M. *Labor and the Left.* See **853.**

1690 LATIMER, Murray W. *Industrial Pensions Systems in the United States.* 2 vols. New York, 1932.

1691 LAUCK, W. Jett, and Edgar SYDENSTRICKER. *Condition of Labor in American Industries.* New York, 1917.

1692 LEIBY, James. *Carroll Wright and Labor Reform: The Origin of Labor Statistics.* Cambridge, Mass., 1960.

1693 LESCOHIER, Don D. *The Labor Market.* New York, 1919.

1694 LESCOHIER, Don D. "Working Conditions." See **60.**

1695 LEVINE, Daniel. "Gompers and Racism: Strategy of Limited Objectives." *Mid-Am,* XLIII (1961), 106–13.

1696 LIEBERMAN, Elias. *Unions Before the Bar.* New York, 1950.

1697 LOMBARDI, John. *Labor's Voice in the Cabinet: A History of the Department of Labor from Its Origin to 1921.* New York, 1942.

1698 LORWIN, Lewis L. *The American Federation of Labor.* Washington, D.C., 1933.

1699 MANDEL, Bernard. *Samuel Gompers.* See **177.**

1700 MANDEL, Bernard. "Samuel Gompers and the Negro Workers, 1886–1914." *J Neg Hist,* XL (1955), 34–60.

1701 MASON, Alpheus T. *Organized Labor and the Law.* Durham, N.C., 1925.

1702 MC LAURIN, Melton A. *Paternalism and Protest: Southern Cotton Mill Workers and Organized Labor, 1875–1905.* Westport, Conn., 1971.

1703 MORE, Louise B. *Wage-Earners' Budgets.* New York, 1907.

1704 MURRAY, Robert K. "Public Opinion, Labor, and the Clayton Act." See **676.**

1705 NADWORTHY, Milton J. *Scientific Management and the Unions, 1900–1932.* Cambridge, Mass., 1955.

1706 NASH, Gerald D. "Franklin D. Roosevelt and Labor: The World War I Origins of the Early New Deal Policy." See **768.**

1707 NELSON, Daniel. *Managers and Workers.* See **1526.**

1708 NELSON, Daniel. "Scientific Management, Systematic Management, and Labor, 1880–1915." See **1527.**

1709 PELLING, Henry. *American Labor.* Chicago, 1960.†

1710 PERLMAN, Mark. *Labor Union Theories in America: Background and Development.* Evanston, Ill., 1958.

1711 PERLMAN, Selig. *A History of Trade Unionism in the United States.* New York, 1922.

1712 PERLMAN, Selig, and Philip TAFT. "Labor Movements, 1896–1932." See **64.**

1713 RAYBACK, Joseph G. *A History of American Labor.* New York, 1959.†

1714 REED, Louis S. *The Labor Philosophy of Samuel Gompers.* New York, 1930.

1715 REES, Albert. *Real Wages in Manufacturing, 1890–1914.* Princeton, 1961.

1716 SAXTON, Alexander. "San Francisco Labor and the Populist and Progressive Insurgencies." See **354.**

1717 SCHEINBERG, Stephen J. "Theodore Roosevelt and the A. F. of L.'s Entry into Politics, 1906–1908." See **571.**

1718 SEIDMAN, Joel. *The Needle Trades.* New York, 1942.

1719 SELEKMAN, Ben M., and Mary VAN KLEECK. *Employees' Representation in Coal Mines.* New York, 1924.

1720 SHAPIRO, Stanley. "The Great War and Reform: Liberals and Labor, 1917–19." See **783.**

1721 SHOVER, John L. "The Progressives and the Working Class Vote in California." See **357.**

1722 SMITH, Darrell Hevenor. *The United States Employment Service.* Baltimore, 1932.

1723 SMITH, Gibbs. *Joe Hill.* See **865.**

1724 SMITH, John S. "Organized Labor and Government in the Wilson Era, 1913–1921: Some Conclusions." See **638.**

1725 STEEL, Edward M. "Mother Jones in the Fairmont Field, 1902." *J Am Hist,* LVII (1970), 290–307.

1726 STEWART, Bryce M., *et al. Unemployment Benefits in the United States.* New York, 1930.

1727 SUFFERN, Arthur E. *Conciliation and Arbitration in the Coal Industry of America.* Boston, 1915.

1728 TAFT, Philip. *The A. F. of L. in the Time of Gompers.* New York, 1957.

1729 TAFT, Philip. "The Federal Trials of the I.W.W." See **788.**

1730 TAFT, Philip. "The I.W.W. in the Grain Belt." *Lab Hist,* I (1960), 53–67.

1731 TAFT, Philip. *Organized Labor in American History.* New York, 1964.

1732 TAYLOR, Albion Guilford. *Labor Policies of the National Association of Manufacturers.* Urbana, Ill., 1928.

1733 TOLMAN, William H. *Social Engineering.* New York, 1909.

1734 TUTTLE, William M., Jr. "Labor Conflict and Racial Violence: The Black Worker in Chicago, 1894–1919." *Lab Hist,* X (1969), 408–32.

1735 TYLER, Robert L. "The I.W.W. and the West." *Am Q,* XII (1960), 175–87.

1736 TYLER, Robert L. *Rebels of the Woods.* See **868.**

1737 VAN TINE, Warren R. *The Making of the Labor Bureaucrat: Union Leadership in the United States, 1870–1920.* Amherst, Mass., 1973.

1738 WAKSTEIN, Allen M. "The Origins of the Open-Shop Movement, 1919–1920." *J Am Hist,* LI (1964), 460–75.

1739 WATKINS, Gordon S. *Labor Problems and Labor Administration in the United States during the World War.* See **799.**

1740 WEINTRAUB, Hyman. *Andrew Furuseth: Emancipator of the Seamen.* Berkeley, 1959.

1741 WEST, George P. *Report on the Colorado Strike.* Washington, D.C., 1915.

1742 WHELPTON, P. K. "Occupational Groups in the United States." *J Am Stat Assn,* XXI (1925), 335–43.

1743 WITTE, Edwin E. *The Government in Labor Disputes.* New York, 1932.

1744 WOLMAN, Leo. *The Boycott in American Trade Unions.* Baltimore, 1916.

1745 WOLMAN, Leo. *The Growth of American Trade Unions, 1880–1923.* New York, 1924.

1746 WOODBURY, Robert M. *Workers' Health and Safety.* New York, 1927.

1747 YELLEN, Samuel. *American Labor Struggles.* New York, 1936.†

1748 YELLOWITZ, Irwin. *Labor and the Progressive Movement in New York City, 1897–1916.* See **376.**

10. Immigrants and Immigration

1749 ADAMIC, Louis. *From Many Lands.* New York, 1940.

1750 ADAMIC, Louis. *A Nation of Nations.* New York, 1945.

1751 ALLSWANG, John M. *A House for All Peoples: Ethnic Politics in Chicago, 1890–1936.* Lexington, Ky., 1971.

1752 BABCOCK, Kendric C. *The Scandinavian Element in the United States.* Urbana, Ill., 1914.

1753 BARRY, Coleman J. *The Catholic Church and German Americans.* Milwaukee, 1953.

1754 BERNARD, William S., ed. *American Immigration Policy: A Reappraisal.* New York, 1950.

1755 BERTHOFF, Rowland T. *British Immigrants in Industrial America, 1790–1950.* Cambridge, Mass., 1953.

1756 BERTHOFF, Rowland T. "Southern Attitudes Toward Immigration, 1865–1914." *J S Hist,* XVII (1951), 328–60.

1757 BOWERS, David F., ed. *Foreign Influences in American Life: Essays and Critical Bibliographies.* Princeton, 1944.

1758 BOYD, Betty. *Italian Repatriation from the United States, 1900–1914.* New York, 1973.

1759 BUROKER, Robert L. "From Voluntary Association to Welfare State: The Illinois Immigrants' Protective League, 1908–1926." *J Am Hist,* LVIII (1971), 643–60.

1760 CARPENTER, Niles. *Immigrants and Their Children, 1920.* Washington, D.C., 1927.

1761 CHILD, Clifton J. *The German–Americans in Politics, 1914–1917.* See **1181.**

1762 CHUDACOFF, Howard P. "A New Look at Ethnic Neighborhoods: Residential Dispersion and the Concept of Visibility in a Medium-Sized City." *J Am Hist,* LX (1973), 76–93.

1763 COMMONS, John R. *Races and Immigrants in America.* New York, 1907.

1764 CURTI, Merle E., and Kendall BIRR. "The Immigrant and the American Image in Europe, 1860–1914." *Miss Val Hist Rev,* XXXVII (1950), 203–30.

1765 DANIELS, Roger. *The Politics of Prejudice.* See **1108.**

1766 FAIRCHILD, Henry P. "The Literacy Test and Its Making." *Q J Econ,* XXXI (1917), 447–60.

1767 FOERSTER, Robert F. *The Italian Immigration of Our Times. Harvard University Economic Studies,* XX (1919).

1768 GARIS, Roy L. *Immigration Restriction.* New York, 1927.

1769 GORDON, Milton M. "Assimilation in America: Theory and Reality." *Daedalus,* XC (1961), 263–85.

1770 GREENE, Victor. *For God and Country: The Rise of Polish and Lithuanian Ethnic Consciousness in America, 1860–1910.* Madison, Wis., 1975.

1771 HANDLIN, Oscar. *The American People in the Twentieth Century.* Cambridge, Mass., 1954.

1772 HANDLIN, Oscar. "American Views of the Jew at the Opening of the Twentieth Century." *Pub Am Jew Hist Soc,* XL (1951), 323–44.

1773 HANDLIN, Oscar. *Race and Nationality in American Life.* New York, 1957.

1774 HANDLIN, Oscar. *The Uprooted.* Boston, 1951.†

1775 HANSEN, Marcus L. *The Immigrant in American History.* Cambridge, Mass., 1940.

1776 HANSEN, Marcus L. *The Mingling of Canadian and American Peoples.* New Haven, 1940.

1777 HEALD, Morrell. "Business Attitudes Toward European Immigration, 1880–1900." *J Econ Hist,* XIII (1953), 291–304.

1778 HIGHAM, John. *Strangers in the Land.* See **53.**

1779 HOUCHINS, Lee, and Chang-su HOUCHINS. "The Korean Experience in America, 1903–1924." *Pac Hist Rev,* XLIII (1974), 548–75.

1780 HOGLUND, A. William. *Finnish Immigrants in America, 1880–1920.* Madison, Wis., 1960.

1781 ICHIHASHI, Yamato. *Japanese in the United States.* Stanford, 1932.

1782 JENKS, Jeremiah W., and W. Jett LAUCK. *The Immigrant Problem.* 5th ed. New York, 1922.

1783 JOHNSON, Stanley C. *A History of Immigration from the United Kingdom to North America, 1763–1912.* London, 1913.

1784 JONES, Maldwyn Allen. *American Immigration.* Chicago, 1960.†

1785 KESSNER, Thomas. *The Golden Door: Italian and Jewish Immigrant Mobility in New York, City, 1885–1915.* New York, 1977.

1786 LEISERSON, William M. *Adjusting Immigrant and Industry.* New York, 1924.

1787 LINKH, Richard M. *American Catholicism and European Immigrants.* Staten Island, N.Y., 1975.

1788 LUEBKE, Frederick C. *Bonds of Loyalty: German Americans and World War I.* See **762.**

1789 MATTHEWS, Fred H. "White Community and 'Yellow Peril.' " *Miss Val Hist Rev,* L (1964), 612–33.

1790 MC CLELLAN, Robert. *The Heathen Chinee: A Study of American Attitudes Toward China, 1890–1905.* Columbus, Ohio, 1971.

1791 MILLER, Herbert A. *The School and the Immigrant.* Cleveland, 1916.

1792 MILLIS, Harry A. *The Japanese Problem in the United States.* New York, 1915.

1793 NELLI, Humbert S. *Italians in Chicago, 1880–1930: A Study in Ethnic Mobility.* New York, 1970.

1794 NELSON, Clifford L. *German–American Political Behavior in Nebraska and Wisconsin, 1916–1920.* Lincoln, Neb., 1972.

1795 PARK, Robert W., and Herbert A. MILLER. *Old World Traits Transplanted.* New York, 1921.

1796 SALOUTOS, Theodore. *The Greeks in the United States.* Cambridge, Mass., 1964.

1797 SALOUTOS, Theodore. *They Remember America: The Story of the Repatriated Greek–Americans.* Berkeley, 1956.

1798 SMITH, Timothy L. "Immigrant Social Aspiration and American Education, 1880–1930." *Am Q,* XXI (1969), 523–43.

1799 SMITH, William C. *Americans in the Making: The Natural History of the Assimilation of Immigrants.* New York, 1939.

1800 STEPHENSON, George M. *A History of American Immigration, 1820–1924.* Boston, 1926.

1801 TAYLOR, Joseph H. "The Restriction of European Immigration, 1890–1924." Doctoral dissertation, University of California, 1936.

1802 THOMAS, William I., and Florian ZNANIECKI. *The Polish Peasant in Europe and America.* 2 vols. New York, 1927.

1803 VECOLI, Rudolph J. "Cantadini in Chicago: A Critique of the Uprooted." *J Am Hist,* LI (1964), 404–17.

1804 WEFALD, Jon. *A Voice of Protest: Norwegians in American Politics, 1890–1917.* Northfield, Minn., 1971.

1805 WILLCOX, Walter F. "The Distribution of Immigrants in the United States." *Q J Econ,* XX (1906), 523–46.

1806 WITTKE, Carl. *The German-Language Press in America.* Lexington, Ky., 1957.

1807 WITTKE, Carl. *The Irish in America.* Baton Rouge, 1956.

1808 WITTKE, Carl. *We Who Built America.* Rev. ed. Cleveland, 1964.

1809 WOOFTER, Thomas J. *Races and Ethnic Groups in American Life.* New York, 1933.

V. Social and Intellectual Main Currents in American Life

1. Social Trends and Changes

1810 ATHERTON, Lewis E. *Main Street on the Middle Border.* Bloomington, Ind., 1954.†

1811 BABER, Ray E., and Edward A. ROSS. *Changes in Size of American Families in One Generation.* Madison, Wis., 1924.

1812 BOORSTIN, Daniel J. *The Americans: The Democratic Experience.* New York, 1973.†

1813 BOWERS, William L. *The Country Life Movement in America, 1900–1970.* Port Washington, N.Y., 1974.

1814 BOWERS, William L. "Country Life Reform, 1900–1920: A Neglected Aspect of Progressive Era History." *Ag Hist,* XLV (1971), 211–21.

1815 BRECKINRIDGE, Sophonisba. *Women in the Twentieth Century.* New York, 1933.

1816 BREMNER, Robert H., *et al.,* eds. *Children and Youth in America: A Documentary History.* 2 vols. Cambridge, Mass., 1970–1971.

1817 BURNHAM, John C. "The Progressive Era Revolution in American Attitudes Toward Sex." *J Am Hist,* LIX (1973), 885–908.

1818 BUSBEY, Katherine G. *Home Life in America.* New York, 1910.

1819 DULLES, Foster Rhea. *America Learns to Play.* New York, 1940.†

1820 HALL, Frederick S., and Elisabeth W. BROOKE. *American Marriage Laws.* New York, 1919.

1821 LE WARNE, Charles P. *Utopias on Puget Sound, 1885–1915.* Seattle, 1975.

1822 LORD, Walter. *The Good Years: From 1900 to the First World War.* New York, 1960.†

1823 LOU, Herbert H. *Juvenile Courts in the United States.* Chapel Hill, 1927.

1824 MANGOLD, George B. *Problems of Child Welfare.* New York, 1914.

1825 MAY, Henry F. *The End of American Innocence: A Study of the First Years of Our Own Time, 1912–1917.* New York, 1959.†

1826 MC GOVERN, James R. "The American Woman's Pre-World War I Freedom in Manners and Morals." *J Am Hist,* LV (1968), 315–33.

1827 MOLINE, Norman T. *Mobility and the Small Town, 1900–1930: Transportation Change in Oregon, Illinois.* Chicago, 1971.

1828 MORRIS, Lloyd R. *Postscript to Yesterday: American Life and Thought, 1896–1946.* New York, 1947.

1829 O'NEILL, William L. *Divorce in the Progressive Era.* New Haven, 1967.†

1830 O'NEILL, William L. "Divorce in the Progressive Era." *Am Q,* XVII (1965), 203–17.

1831 O'NEILL, William L. *Everyone Was Brave: The Rise and Fall of Feminism in America.* Chicago, 1969.†

1832 POTTER, David M. *People of Plenty.* Chicago, 1954.†

1833 SEYMOUR, Harold. *Baseball: The Golden Age* [1903–1930]. New York, 1971.

1834 SMUTS, Robert W. *Women and Work in America.* New York, 1959.

1835 STIGLER, George J. *Domestic Servants in the United States, 1900–1940.* New York, 1946.

1836 THOMAS, William I., and Florian ZNANIECKI. *The Polish Peasant in Europe and America.* See **1802.**

2. Currents of American Thought

1837 AARON, Daniel. *Men of Good Hope.* See **486**.

1838 ADAMS, Henry. *The Education of Henry Adams.* New York, 1918.†

1839 BARKER, Charles A. *Henry George.* See **83**.

1840 BOURKE, Paul F. "The Social Critics and the End of American Innocence: 1907–1912." *J Am Stud,* III (1969), 57–72.

1841 BOURKE, Paul F. "The Status of Politics 1909–1919: *The New Republic,* Randolph Bourne and Van Wyck Brooks." See **488**.

1842 CARGILL, Oscar. *Intellectual America.* New York, 1941.

1843 COMMAGER, Henry S. *The American Mind.* See **489**.

1844 CURTI, Merle E. *The Growth of American Thought.* See **490**.

1845 CYWAR, Alan. "John Dewey: Toward Domestic Reconstruction, 1915–1920." See **491**.

1846 DORFMAN, Joseph. *The Economic Mind in American Civilization.* See **493**.

1847 DORFMAN, Joseph. *Thorstein Veblen and His America.* See **494**.

1848 DUDDEN, Arthur P. *Joseph Fels and the Single-Tax Movement.* Philadelphia, 1971.

1849 DYKHUIZEN, George. *The Life and Mind of John Dewey.* Carbondale, Ill., 1973.

1850 EKIRCH, Arthur A., Jr. *The Decline of American Liberalism.* New York, 1955.

1851 FARRELL, John C. "John Dewey and World War I: Armageddon Tests a Liberal's Faith." *Perspectives in American History,* IX (1975), 299–342.

1852 FORD, Worthington D., ed. *Letters of Henry Adams, 1892–1918.* Boston, 1938.

1853 FOX, Daniel M. *Discovery of Abundance.* See **496**.

1854 GABRIEL, Ralph H. *The Course of American Democratic Thought.* See **497**.

1855 GILBERT, James. *Designing the Industrial State: The Intellectual Pursuit of Collectivism in America, 1880–1940.* Chicago, 1972.

1856 GRAYBAR, Lloyd J. *Albert Shaw of the Review of Reviews.* See **130**.

1857 HOFSTADTER, Richard. *The Progressive Historians.* See **500**.

1858 HOFSTADTER, Richard. *Social Darwinism in American Thought, 1860–1915.* Philadelphia, 1944.†

1859 HOOK, Sidney. *John Dewey.* See **501**.

1860 JOOST, Nicholas. *Years of Transition: The Dial, 1912–1920.* Barre, 1967.

1861 MANE, Robert. *Henry Adams on the Road to Chartres.* Cambridge, Mass., 1971.

1862 MARCELL, David W. *Progress and Pragmatism: James, Dewey, Beard, and the American Idea of Progress.* Westport, Conn., 1974.

1863 MAY, Henry. "The Rebellion of the Intellectuals, 1912–1917." *Am Q,* VIII (1956), 114–26.

1864 MC CLOSKEY, Robert G. *American Conservatism in the Age of Enterprise: A Study of William Graham Sumner, Stephen J. Field, and Andrew Carnegie.* Cambridge, Mass., 1951.

1865 PERRY, Ralph Barton. *The Thought and Character of William James.* 2 vols. Boston, 1935.

1866 PICKENS, Donald K. *Eugenics and Progressives.* See **506.**

1867 QUANDT, Jean B. *From the Small Town to the Great Community.* See **507.**

1868 RUCKER, Darnell. *The Chicago Pragmatists.* Minneapolis, 1969.

1869 SCHNEIDER, Herbert W. *A History of American Philosophy.* 2nd ed. New York, 1963.†

1870 WILD, John. *The Radical Empiricism of William James.* Garden City, N.Y., 1969.

1871 WHITE, Morton. *Social Thought in America.* See **511.**

3. Education

1872 BARNARD, John. *From Evangelicalism to Progressivism at Oberlin College, 1866–1917.* See **431.**

1873 BECK, Holmes. "American Progressive Education, 1875–1930." Doctoral Dissertation, Yale University, 1941.

1874 BILLINGTON, Ray Allen. *Frederick Jackson Turner: Historian, Scholar, Teacher.* New York, 1973.

1875 BILLINGTON, Ray Allen. "Tempest in Clio's Teapot: The American Historical Association Rebellion of 1915." *Am Hist Rev,* LXXVIII (1973), 348–69.

1876 BURNS, Edward M. *David Starr Jordan.* Stanford, 1953.

1877 BUTLER, Nicholas Murray. *Across the Busy Years.* 2 vols. New York, 1939–1940.

1878 BUTTS, R. Freeman, and Lawrence A. CREMIN. *A History of Education in American Culture.* New York, 1953.

1879 CREMIN, Lawrence A. *The Transformation of the School: Progressivism in American Education, 1876–1957.* New York, 1961.†

1880 CUBBERLY, Ellwood P. *Changing Conceptions of Education.* Boston, 1909.

1881 CUBBERLY, Ellwood P. *Public Education in the United States.* Boston, 1919.

1882 CURTI, Merle E. "The American Scholar in Three Wars." *J Hist Ideas,* III (1942), 241–64.

1883 CURTI, Merle E. *The Social Ideas of American Educators.* New York, 1935.

1884 CURTI, Merle E., and Vernon CARSTENSEN. *The University of Wisconsin: A History, 1848–1925.* Madison, Wis., 1949.

1885 DABNEY, Charles W. *Universal Education in the South.* 2 vols. Chapel Hill, 1936.

1886 FRENCH, John C. *A History of the University Founded by Johns Hopkins.* Baltimore, 1946.

1887 GRUBER, Carol S. *Mars and Minerva.* See **738.**

1888 HAWKINS, Hugh. "Charles W. Eliot, University Reform and Religious Faith in America, 1869–1909." *J Am Hist,* LI (1964), 191–213.

1889 HERBST, Jurgen. *The German Historical School in American Scholarship: A Study in the Transfer of Culture.* Ithaca, N.Y., 1965.

1890 HOLT, W. Stull, ed. *Historical Scholarship in the United States, 1876–1901: As Revealed in the Correspondence of Herbert B. Adams.* Baltimore, 1938.

1891 HOOK, Sidney. *John Dewey.* See **501.**

1892 KANDEL, I. L. *American Education in the Twentieth Century.* Cambridge, Mass., 1957.

1893 KNIGHT, Edgar W. *Fifty Years of American Education, 1900–1950.* New York, 1952.

1894 LAZERSON, Marvin. *Origins of the Urban School: Public Education in Massachusetts, 1870–1915.* Cambridge, Mass., 1971.

1895 MC PHERSON, James M. "White Liberals and Black Power in Negro Education, 1865–1915." *Am Hist Rev,* LXXV (1970), 1357–79.

1896 MIMS, Edwin. *Chancellor Kirkland of Vanderbilt.* Nashville, Tenn., 1940.

1897 MOORE, Ernest C. *Fifty Years of American Education.* Boston, 1917.

1898 MORISON, Samuel E., ed. *The Development of Harvard University since the Inauguration of President Eliot, 1869–1929.* Cambridge, Mass., 1930.

1899 NETHERS, John L. *Simeon D. Fess: Educator & Politician.* Brooklyn, 1973.

1900 NOBLE, Stuart G. *A History of American Education.* New York, 1953.

1901 OSBURN, W. J. *Foreign Criticisms of American Education.* Washington, D.C., 1922.

1902 PIERSON, George W. *Yale College: An Educational History, 1871–1921.* New Haven, 1952.

1903 ROSSI, Peter H., and Alice S. ROSSI. "Some Effects of Parochial-School Education in America." *Daedalus,* XC (1961), 300–28.

1904 RUGG, Harold. *Foundations for American Education.* Yonkers-on-Hudson, N.Y., 1947.

1905 SCHLIPP, Paul A., ed. *The Philosophy of John Dewey.* Evanston, Ill., 1939.

1906 SIZER, Theodore R. *Secondary Schools at the Turn of the Century.* New Haven, 1964.

1907 SMITH, Timothy L. "Immigrant Social Aspirations and American Education, 1880–1930." See **1798.**

1908 TYACK, David B. *The One Best System: A History of American Urban Education.* Cambridge, Mass., 1974.†

1909 VAN TASSEL, David D. "The American Historical Association and the South, 1884–1913." *J S Hist,* XXIII (1957), 465–82.

1910 VEYSEY, Laurence R. *The Emergence of the American University.* Chicago, 1965.†

1911 WILSON, Louis R. *The University of North Carolina, 1900–1930: The Making of a Modern University.* Chapel Hill, 1957.

1912 WOYTANOWITZ, George M. *University Extension: The Early Years in the United States, 1885–1915.* Iowa City, 1975.

1913 YEOMANS, Henry A. *Abbott Lawrence Lowell, 1856–1943.* Cambridge, Mass., 1948.

4. Science, Medicine, and Public Health

1914 BENISON, Saul. "The Enigma of Poliomyelitis: 1910." *Freedom and Reform: Essays in Honor of Henry Steele Commager.* Eds. Harold M. Hyman and Leonard W. Levy. New York, 1967.

1915 BUCKLER, Helen. *Daniel Hale Williams, Negro Surgeon.* New York, 1968.

1916 BURNHAM, John C. *Psychoanalysis and American Medicine, 1894–1918.* New York, 1967.

1917 CLAPESATTLE, Helen. *The Doctors Mayo.* Minneapolis, 1941.†

1918 DANIELS, George H. *Science in American Society: A Social History.* New York, 1971.

1919 DE KRUIF, Paul. *Microbe Hunters.* New York, 1926.

1920 DEUTSCH, Albert. *The Mentally Ill in America: A History of Their Care and Treatment from Colonial Times.* Rev. ed. New York, 1946.

1921 DUPREE, A. Hunter, ed. *Science and the Emergence of Modern America, 1865–1916.* Chicago, 1963.

1922 DUPREE, A. Hunter. *Science in the Federal Government: A History of Policies and Activities to 1940.* Cambridge, Mass., 1957.

1923 FLEMING, Donald. *William H. Welch and the Rise of Modern Medicine.* Boston, 1954.†

1924 FLEXNER, Simon, and J. T. FLEXNER. *William Henry Welch and the Heroic Age of American Medicine.* New York, 1941.

1925 GALISHOFF, Stuart. *Safeguarding the Public Health: Newark, 1895–1918.* Westport, Conn., 1975.

1926 HALE, Nathan G., Jr. *Freud and the Americans: The Beginnings of Psychoanalysis in the United States, 1876–1917.* New York, 1971.

1927 HARROW, Benjamin. *Vitamins.* New York, 1921.

1928 KELVES, Daniel J. "George Ellery Hale, the First World War, and the Advancement of Science in America." See **753.**

1929 KEVLES, Daniel J. "Testing the Army's Intelligence: Psychologists and the Military in World War I." See **754.**

1930 LAYTON, Edwin T., Jr. *The Revolt of the Engineers: Social Responsibility and the American Engineering Profession.* Cleveland, 1971.

1931 LEIGH, Robert D. *Federal Health Administration.* New York, 1927.

1932 ROBERTS, Mary M. *American Nursing: History and Interpretation.* New York, 1954.

1933 RODGERS, Andrew D., III. *Liberty Hyde Bailey.* Princeton, 1949.

1934 SHRYOCK, Richard H. *American Medical Research.* New York, 1947.

1935 SHRYOCK, Richard H. *The Development of Modern Medicine.* New York, 1947.

1936 TOBEY, James A. *The National Government and Public Health.* Baltimore, 1926.

1937 YOUNG, James H. *The Medical Messiahs: A Social History of Health Quackery in Twentieth-Century America.* Princeton, 1967.†

5. Religion

1938 ABRAMS, Ray H. *Preachers Present Arms.* See **695.**

1939 ABELL, Aaron I. *American Catholicism and Social Action.* See **427.**

1940 ABELL, Aaron I. "The Religious Aspect of American Life." *Rev Pol,* XXI (1959), 24–52.

1941 ABELL, Aaron I. *The Urban Impact on American Protestantism, 1865–1900.* See **428.**

1942 AHLSTROM, Sydney E. *A Religious History of the American People.* New Haven, 1972.†

1943 ARMSTRONG, Maurice W., *et al.,* eds. *The Presbyterian Enterprise: Sources of American Presbyterian History.* Philadelphia, 1956.

1944 BAILEY, Kenneth K. *Southern White Protestantism in the Twentieth Century.* New York, 1964.

1945 BARKER, John M. *The Social Gospel and the New Era.* See **430.**

1946 BARNARD, John. *From Evangelicalism to Progressivism at Oberlin College, 1866–1917.* See **431.**

1947 BARRY, Coleman J. *The Catholic Church and German–Americans.* See **1753.**

1948 BODE, Frederick A. *Protestantism and the New South: North Carolina Baptists and Methodists in Political Crisis, 1894–1903.* Charlottesville, Va., 1976.

1949 BOWDEN, Henry W. *Church History in the Age of Science: Historiographical Patterns in the United States, 1876–1918.* Chapel Hill, 1971.

1950 BRAUER, Jerald C. *Protestantism in America.* Rev. ed., Philadelphia, 1966.†

1951 CUDDY, Edward. "Pro-Germanism and American Catholicism, 1914–1917." See **1186.**

1952 DORN, Jacob H. *Washington Gladden.* See **432.**

1953 EIGHMY, John L. "Religious Liberalism in the South during the Progressive Era." *Church Hist,* XXXVIII (1969), 359–72.

1954 ELLIS, John Tracy. *American Catholicism.* 2nd ed. Chicago, 1969.†

1955 ELLIS, John Tracy. *The Life of James Cardinal Gibbons.* 2 vols. Milwaukee, 1952.

1956 FISH, John O. "Southern Methodism and Accomodation of the Negro, 1902–1915." *J Neg Hist,* LV (1970), 200–14.

1957 FURNISS, Norman F. *The Fundamentalist Controversy, 1918–1931.* New Haven, 1954.

1958 GAUSTAD, Edwin S. *A Religious History of America.* New York, 1967.

1959 GLAZER, Nathan. *American Judaism.* Rev. ed. Chicago, 1972.†

1960 GOTTSCHALK, Stephen. *The Emergence of Christian Science in American Religious Life.* Berkeley, 1973.

1961 HANDY, Robert T. "Christianity and Socialism in America, 1900–1920." See **849.**

1962 HERBERG, Will. *Protestant, Catholic, Jew.* Garden City, N.Y., 1955.†

1963 HOPKINS, Charles H. *History of the Y.M.C.A. in North America.* New York, 1951.

1964 HOPKINS, Charles H. *The Rise of the Social Gospel in American Protestantism, 1865–1915.* See **433.**

1965 HUDSON, Winthrop S. *American Protestantism.* Chicago, 1961.†

1966 KNOX, Israel. *Rabbi In America: The Story of Isaac M. Wise.* Boston, 1957.

1967 LANKFORD, John E. "The Impact of the New Era Movement on the Presbyterian Church in the United States of America, 1918–1925." *J Presby Hist,* XL (1962), 213–24.

1968 MAY, Henry F. *Protestant Churches and Industrial America.* See **434.**

1969 MAYNARD, Theodore. *The Story of American Catholicism.* New York, 1943.

1970 MC AVOY, Thomas T. "The Catholic Minority after the Americanist Controversy, 1899–1917: A Survey." *Rev Pol,* XXI (1959), 53–82.

1971 MC AVOY, Thomas T. *A History of the Catholic Church in the United States.* Notre Dame, Ind., 1969.

1972 MILLER, Robert Moats. "Methodism and American Society, 1900–1939." See **435.**

1973 MOYNIHAN, James H. *The Life of Archbishop John Ireland.* New York, 1953.

1974 OLMSTEAD, Clifton E. *History of Religion in the United States.* Englewood Cliffs, N.J., 1960.

1975 RAUSCHENBUSCH, Walter. *Christianity and the Social Crisis.* See **437.**

1976 RAUSCHENBUSCH, Walter. *A Theology for the Social Gospel.* See **438.**

1977 SAPPINGTON, Roger E. *Brethren Social Policy, 1908–1958.* See **439.**

1978 SCHNEIDER, Herbert W. *Religion in 20th Century America.* Cambridge, Mass., 1952.

1979 SMITH, James W., and A. Leland JAMISON, eds. *Religion in American Life.* 4 vols. Princeton, 1961.†

1980 SPERRY, Willard L. *Religion in America.* Cambridge, Mass., 1946.

1981 STELZLE, Charles. *American Social and Religious Conditions.* See **441.**

1982 SWEET, William W. *The Story of Religion in America.* Rev. ed. New York, 1950.†

1983 WELCH, Richard E., Jr. "Organized Religion and the Philippine–American War, 1899–1902." See **978.**

1984 WILLIAMS, Michael. *American Catholics in the War.* See **804.**

1985 WISBEY, Herbert A., Jr. *Soldiers Without Swords: A History of the Salvation Army in the United States.* New York, 1955.

6. The Arts

1986 BAIGELL, Matthew. *A History of American Painting.* New York, 1971.

1987 BARKER, Virgil. *American Painting, History, and Interpretation.* New York, 1950.

1988 BOGAN, Louise. *Achievement in American Poetry, 1900–1950.* Chicago, 1951.†

1989 BROOKS, Van Wyck. *The Confident Years, 1885–1915.* New York, 1952.

1990 BROOKS, Van Wyck. *New England: Indian Summer.* New York, 1940.

1991 CHASE, Gilbert. *America's Music.* Rev. ed. New York, 1966.

1992 CONDIT, Carl W. *American Building Art.* 2 vols. New York, 1960–1961.

1993 CONDIT, Carl W. *Chicago, 1910–29: Building, Planning, and Urban Technology.* Chicago, 1973.†

1994 CONDIT, Carl W. *The Rise of the Skyscraper.* Chicago, 1952.

1995 CULSHAW, John. *A Century of Music.* London, 1952.

1996 DOWNER, Alan S. *Fifty Years of American Drama, 1900–1950.* Chicago, 1951.

1997 EATON, Leonard K. *Two Chicago Architects and Their Clients: Frank Lloyd Wright and Howard Van Doren Shaw.* Cambridge, Mass., 1969.†

1998 FITCH, James M. *American Building.* Boston, 1948.

1999 GEISMAR, Maxwell D. *The Last of the Provincials: The American Novel, 1915–1925.* Boston, 1947.

2000 GEISMAR, Maxwell D. *Rebels and Ancestors: The Modern American Novel, 1890–1915.* Boston, 1953.

2001 GESELBRACHT, Raymond H. "Transcendental Renaissance in the Arts: 1890–1920." *N Eng Q,* XLVIII (1975), 463–86.

2002 GLICKSBERG, Charles E., ed. *American Literary Criticism, 1900–1950.* New York, 1952.

2003 GREGORY, Horace, and Marya ZATURENSKA. *A History of American Poetry, 1900–1940.* New York, 1946.

2004 GRIFFITH, Linda A. *When the Movies Were Young.* New York, 1925.

2005 HICKS, Granville. *The Great Tradition: An Interpretation of American Literature Since the Civil War.* Rev. ed. New York, 1935.

2006 HINES, Thomas S. "The Paradox of 'Progressive' Architecture: Urban Planning and Public Building in Tom Johnson's Cleveland." *Am Q,* XXV (1973), 426–48.

2007 HOFFMAN, Frederick J. *The Modern Novel in America, 1900–1950.* Rev. ed. Chicago, 1964.†

2008 HOMER, William I. *Robert Henri and His Circle.* Ithaca, N.Y., 1969.

2009 HOWARD, John T. *Our American Music.* Rev. ed. New York, 1946.

2010 HOWARD, John T. *Our Contemporary Composers.* New York, 1941.

2011 HOWARD, Leon. *Literature and the American Tradition.* Garden City, N.Y., 1960.

2012 KAZIN, Alfred. *On Native Grounds: An Interpretation of Modern American Prose Literature.* New York, 1942.†

2013 LARKIN, Oliver. *Art and Life in America.* New York, 1949.

2014 MATHEWS, Marcia M. *Henry Ossawa Tanner: American Artist.* Chicago, 1969.

2015 O'CONNOR, William V. *An Age of Criticism, 1900–1950.* Chicago, 1952.†

2016 PHELPS, William L. *The Twentieth Century Theatre.* New York, 1918.

2017 RIDEOUT, Walter B. *The Radical Novel in the United States, 1900–1954.* Cambridge, Mass., 1956.†

2018 ROSSITER, Frank R. *Charles Ives and His America.* New York, 1975.

2019 SCHNEIDER, Robert W. *Five Novelists of the Progressive Era.* New York, 1965.

2020 SINCLAIR, Upton. *Autobiography.* See **457.**

2021 SPAETH, Sigmund G. *A History of Popular Music in America.* New York, 1948.

2022 SPILLER, Robert E., *et al.,* eds. *Literary History of the United States.* See **30.**

2023 TAYLOR, Walter F. *The Economic Novel in America.* Chapel Hill, 1942.

2024 THORP, Willard. *American Writing in the Twentieth Century.* Cambridge, Mass., 1960.

2025 WRIGHT, Frank Lloyd. *An Autobiography.* London, 1932.

2026 WRIGHT, Frank Lloyd. *Modern Architecture.* Princeton, 1931.

7. *Journalism*

2027 BAKER, Ray Stannard. *American Chronicle.* See **79.**

2028 BANNISTER, Robert C., Jr. *Ray Stannard Baker.* See **82.**

2029 BAUMGARTNER, Apollinaris W. *Catholic Journalism: A Study of Its Development in the U.S., 1789–1930.* New York, 1931.

2030 BLEYER, Willard G. *Main Currents in the History of American Journalism.* Boston, 1927.

2031 BRITT, George. *Forty Years—Forty Millions: The Career of Frank A. Munsey.* New York, 1935.

2032 BROWN, Charles H. *The Correspondents' War: Journalists in the Spanish–American War.* New York, 1972.

2033 BROWN, Dorothy M. "The Quality Magazines in the Progressive Era." *Mid-Am,* LIII (1971), 139–59.

2034 COCHRAN, Negley D. *E. W. Scripps.* New York, 1933.

2035 CONLIN, Joseph R. *The American Radical Press, 1880–1960.* See **839.**

2036 CREEL, George. *Rebel at Large.* See **104.**

2037 DABNEY, Thomas E. *One Hundred Great Years: The Story of the Times–Picayune From Its Founding to 1940.* Baton Rouge, 1944.

2038 DANIELS, Josephus. *Editor in Politics.* See **108.**

2039 DANIELS, Josephus. *Tar Heel Editor.* See **109.**

2040 ELLIS, Elmer. *Mr. Dooley's America.* See **112.**

2041 GRAYBAR, Lloyd J. *Albert Shaw of the* Review of Reviews. See **130.**

2042 HARRIS, Leon. *Upton Sinclair.* See **141.**

2043 HEATON, John L. *Cobb of "The World."* New York, 1924.

2044 JOHNSON, Walter. *William Allen White's America.* See **153.**

2045 KAPLAN, Justin. *Lincoln Steffens.* See **154.**

2046 LYON, Peter. *Success Story.* See **452.**

2047 MC KEE, John D. *William Allen White.* See **184.**

2048 MORRISON, Joseph L. *Josephus Daniels Says. . . . : An Editor's Political Odyssey from Bryan to Wilson and F.D.R., 1894–1913.* Chapel Hill, 1962.

2049 MOTT, Frank L. *American Journalism.* See **453.**

2050 MOTT, Frank L. *A History of American Magazines.* See **454.**

2051 NEVINS, Allan. *The Letters and Journal of Brand Whitlock.* See **187.**

2052 NOBLE, David W. "The New Republic and the Idea of Progress, 1914–1920." See **505.**

2053 OLDER, Fremont. *William Randolph Hearst.* See **190.**

2054 PETERSON, Theodore. *Magazines in the Twentieth Century.* Urbana, Ill., 1956.

2055 STEFFENS, Lincoln. *The Autobiography of Lincoln Steffens.* See **212.**

2056 SULLIVAN, Mark. *The Education of an American.* See **215.**

2057 SWANBERG, W. A. *Citizen Hearst.* See **216.**

2058 SWANBERG, W. A. *Pulitzer.* See **217.**

2059 THORNBROUGH, Emma Lou. "American Negro Newspapers, 1880–1914." *Bus Hist Rev,* XL (1966), 467–90.

2060 THORNBROUGH, Emma Lou. *T. Thomas Fortune: Militant Journalist.* Chicago, 1972.

2061 VILLARD, Oswald Garrison. *Fighting Years.* See **222.**

2062 WATTERSON, Henry. *"Marse Henry."* See **227.**

2063 WHITE, William Allen. *The Autobiography of William Allen White.* See **229.**

2064 WILSON, Harold S. *McClure's Magazine and the Muckrakers.* See **459.**

2065 WINTER, Ella, and Granville HICKS, eds. *The Letters of Lincoln Steffens.* See **230.**

2066 WITTKE, Carl. *The German-Language Press in America.* See **1806.**

2067 WOOD, James P. *Magazines in the United States.* New York, 1949.

8. The Negro

2068 ALLEN, Howard W., Aage R. CLAUSEN, and Jerome M. CLUBB. "Political Reform and Negro Rights in the Senate, 1909–1915." *J S Hist,* XXXVII (1971), 191–212.

2069 APTHEKER, Herbert, ed. *The Correspondence of W. E. B. DuBois.* See **77.**

2070 ATHEY, Louis L. "Florence Kelley and the Quest for Negro Equality." See **382.**

2071 BARBEAU, Arthur E., and Florette HENRI. *The Unknown Soldiers.* See **699.**

SOCIAL AND INTELLECTUAL MAIN CURRENTS

2072 BERRY, Mary F. *Black Resistance, White Law: A History of Constitutional Racism in America.* New York, 1971.†

2073 BERRY, Mary F. "Reparations for Freedom, 1890–1916: Fradulent Practices or Justice Deferred?" *J Neg Hist,* LVII (1972), 219–30.

2074 BLUMENTHAL, Henry. "Woodrow Wilson and the Race Question." See **648.**

2075 BRODERICK, Francis L. *W. E. B. DuBois.* See **92.**

2076 BUCKLER, Helen. *Daniel Hale Williams.* See **1915.**

2077 BUNI, Andrew. *The Negro in Virginia Politics, 1902–1965.* Charlottesville, Va., 1967.

2078 CALLCOTT, Margaret L. *The Negro in Maryland Politics, 1870–1912.* Baltimore, 1969.

2079 Chicago Commission on Race Relations. *The Negro in Chicago.* See **713.**

2080 CROWE, Charles. "Racial Violence and Social Reform—Origins of the Atlanta Riot of 1906." *J Neg Hist,* LIII (1968), 234–56.

2081 DANIEL, Pete. "Up From Slavery and Down to Peonage: The Alonzo Bailey Case." *J Am Hist,* LVII (1970), 654–70.

2082 EDMONDS, Helen G. *The Negro and Fusion Politics in North Carolina, 1894–1901.* Chapel Hill, 1951.

2083 FISH, John O. "Southern Methodism and Accomodation of the Negro, 1902–1915." See **1956.**

2084 FOX, Stephen R. *The Guardian of Boston: William Monroe Trotter.* New York, 1970.

2085 FRANKLIN, John Hope. *From Slavery to Freedom.* See **46.**

2086 FRAZIER, E. Franklin. *The Negro Family in the United States.* Chicago, 1939.†

2087 GATEWOOD, Willard B., Jr. "Black Americans and the Quest for Empire, 1898–1903." See **939.**

2088 GATEWOOD, Willard B. Jr. *Black Americans and the White Man's Burden, 1898–1903.* See **940.**

2089 GREENE, Lorenzo J., and Carter G. WOODSON. *The Negro Wage Earner.* Washington, D.C., 1930.

2090 HARLAN, Louis R. *Booker T. Washington.* See **139.**

2091 HARLAN, Louis R. "Booker T. Washington in Biographical Perspective." *Am Hist Rev,* LXXV (1970), 1581–99.

2092 HARLAN, Louis R., *et al.,* eds. *The Booker T. Washington Papers.* See **140.**

2093 HARLAN, Louis R. "The Secret Life of Booker T. Washington." *J S Hist,* XXXVII (1971), 393–416.

2094 HARLAN, Louis R. *Separate and Unequal: Public School Campaigns and Racism in the Southern Seaboard States, 1901–1915.* Chapel Hill, 1958.

2095 HARRIS, Carl V. "Reforms in Government Control of Negroes in Birmingham, Alabama, 1890–1920." *J S Hist,* XXXVIII (1972), 567–600.

2096 HENRI, Florette. *Black Migration.* See **1405.**

2097 HIGGS, Robert. "The Boll Weevil, the Cotton Economy, and Black Migration, 1910–1930." See **1406.**

86

2098 HOLMES, William F. "Whitecapping: Agrarian Violence in Mississippi, 1902–1906." See **540.**

2099 JACK, Robert L. *History of the National Association for the Advancement of Colored People.* See **259.**

2100 JOHNSON, Charles S. *Patterns of Negro Segregation.* New York, 1943.

2101 JOHNSON, Guion Griffis. "The Ideology of White Supremacy, 1876–1910." *Essays in Southern History Present to Joseph Gregoire de Roulhac Hamilton. . . .* Ed. Fletcher M. Green. Chapel Hill, 1949.

2102 KELLOGG, Charles F. *NAACP.* See **260.**

2103 KENNEDY, Louise V. *The Negro Peasant Turns Cityward.* See **1409.**

2104 KIRBY, J. T. *Darkness at Dawning: Race and Reform in the Progressive South.* Philadelphia, 1972.†

2105 LANE, Ann J. *The Brownsville Affair.* See **549.**

2106 LOGAN, Rayford W. *The Negro in American Life and Thought: The Nadir, 1877–1901.* New York, 1954.†

2107 MANDEL, Bernard. "Samuel Gompers and the Negro Worker, 1886–1914." See **1700.**

2108 MC PHERSON, James M. *The Abolitionist Legacy: From Reconstruction to the NAACP.* Princeton, 1976.†

2109 MC PHERSON, James M. "White Liberals and Black Power in Negro Education, 1865–1915." See **1895.**

2110 MC PHERSON, James M., *et al. Blacks in America: Bibliographical Essays.* See **21.**

2111 MEIER, August. *Negro Thought in America, 1880–1915.* Ann Arbor, Mich., 1963.

2112 MEIER, August. "The Rise of Segregation in the Federal Bureaucracy, 1900–1930." *Phylon,* XXVIII (1967), 178–84.

2113 MEIER, August. "Toward a Reinterpretation of Booker T. Washington." *J S Hist,* XXIII (1957), 220–27.

2114 MEIER, August, and Elliott RUDWICK. "The Boycott Movement Against Jim Crow Streetcars in the South, 1900–1906." *J Am Hist,* LV (1969), 756–75.

2115 MEIER, August, and Elliott M. RUDWICK. *From Plantation to Ghetto.* Rev. ed. New York, 1976.†

2116 MILLER, Sally M. "The Socialist Party and the Negro, 1901–20." See **854.**

2117 MOORE, R. Laurence. "Flawed Fraternity—American Socialist Response to the Negro, 1901–1912." See **858.**

2118 MYRDAL, Gunnar. *An American Dilemma.* 2 vols. New York, 1944.†

2119 NEWBY, I. A. *Black Carolinians: A History of Blacks in South Carolina from 1895 to 1968.* Columbia, S.C., 1973.

2120 NEWBY, I. A. *Jim Crow's Defense: Anti-Negro Thought in America, 1900–1930.* Baton Rouge, 1965.†

2121 REDKEY, Edwin S. *Black Exodus: Black Nationalism and Back-to-Africa Movements, 1890–1910.* New Haven, 1969.

2122 REID, Ira DeA. *The Negro Immigrant.* New York, 1939.

2123 ROSS, Barbara J. *J. E. Spingarn and the Rise of the NAACP, 1911–1939.* New York, 1972.†

2124 ROSS, Frank A., and Louise V. KENNEDY. *A Bibliography of Negro Migration.* New York, 1934.

2125 RUDWICK, Elliott M. *Race Riot at East St. Louis, July 2, 1917.* See **780.**

2126 RUDWICK, Elliott M. *W. E. B. DuBois: A Study in Minority Group Leadership.* Philadelphia, 1960.

2127 SCHEIBER, Jane L., and Harry N. SCHEIBER. "The Wilson Administration and the Wartime Mobilization of Black Americans, 1917–18." See **782.**

2128 SCHEINER, Seth M. *Negro Mecca: A History of the Negro in New York City, 1865–1920.* New York, 1965.†

2129 SCHEINER, Seth M. "President Theodore Roosevelt and the Negro, 1901–1908." See **572.**

2130 SCOTT, Emmet J. *Negro Migration during the War.* New York, 1920.

2131 SCROGGS, William O. "Interstate Migration of Negro Population." *J Pol Econ,* XXV (1917), 1034–43.

2132 SHERMAN, Richard B. *The Republican Party and Black America.* See **573.**

2133 SMITH, T. Lynn. "The Redistribution of the Negro Population in the United States, 1910–1960." *J Neg Hist,* LI (1966), 155–73.

2134 SMITH, Willard H. "William Jennings Bryan and Racism." *J Neg Hist,* LIV (1969), 127–49.

2135 SOCHEN, June. *The Unbridgeable Gap: Blacks and Their Quest for the American Dream, 1900–1930.* Chicago, 1972.†

2136 SOUTHERN, David W. *Malignant Heritage.* See **273.**

2137 SPEAR, Allan H. *Black Chicago: The Making of a Negro Ghetto, 1890–1920.* Chicago, 1967.†

2138 SPENCER, Samuel R., Jr. *Booker T. Washington and the Negro's Place in American Life.* Boston, 1955.†

2139 SPERO, Sterling D., and Abram L. HARRIS. *The Black Worker.* New York, 1931.

2140 THORNBROUGH, Emma Lou. "American Negro Newspapers, 1880–1914." See **2059.**

2141 THORNBROUGH, Emma Lou. *T. Thomas Fortune.* See **2060.**

2142 TUTTLE, William M., Jr. "Labor Conflict and Racial Violence: The Black Worker in Chicago, 1894–1919." See **1734.**

2143 WASHINGTON, Booker T. *Up From Slavery.* See **226.**

2144 WEISS, Nancy J. *The National Urban League, 1910–1940.* New York, 1974.

2145 WEISS, Nancy J. "The Negro and the New Freedom: Fighting Wilsonian Segregation." See **692.**

2146 WESLEY, Charles H. *Negro Labor in the United States.* New York, 1927.

2147 WHITE, Walter. *Rope & Faggot.* New York, 1929.

2148 WILLARD, George-Anne. "Charles Lee Coon: Negro Education and the Atlanta Speech Controversy." *East Carolina College Publications in History,* III (1966), 151–74.

2149 WISEMAN, John B. "Racism in Democratic Politics, 1904–1912." See **585.**

2150 WISH, Harvey. "Negro Education and the Progressive Movement." *J Neg Hist,* XLIX (1964), 184–200.

2151 WOLGEMUTH, Kathleen L. "Woodrow Wilson's Appointment Policy and the Negro." See **694.**

2152 WOODWARD, C. Vann. *Origins of the New South, 1877–1913.* See **375.**

2153 WOODWARD, C. Vann. *The Strange Career of Jim Crow.* Rev. ed. New York, 1966.†

2154 WOOFTER, Thomas J. *Negro Migration: Changes in Rural Organization and Population of the Cotton Belt.* New York, 1920.

2155 WYNES, Charles E. *Forgotten Voices: Dissenting Southerners in an Age of Conformity.* Baton Rouge, 1967.

9. Nativism

2156 ALEXANDER, Charles C. *The Ku Klux Klan in the Southwest.* Lexington, Ky., 1965.

2157 ALLPORT, Gordon W. *The Nature of Prejudice.* Boston, 1954.†

2158 AVIN, Benjamin H. "The Ku Klux Klan, 1915–1925: A Study in Religious Intolerance." Doctoral dissertation, Georgetown University, 1952.

2159 BERTHOFF, Rowland T. "Southern Attitudes Toward Immigration, 1865–1914." See **1755.**

2160 BLUM, John M. "Nativism, Anti-Radicalism, and the Foreign Scare, 1917–1920." See **707.**

2161 BOWERS, David F., ed. *Foreign Influences in American Life.* See **1757.**

2162 CHAFEE, Zechariah, Jr. *Free Speech in the United States.* See **711.**

2163 CHALMERS, David M. *Hooded Americanism: The First Century of the Ku Klux Klan, 1865–1965.* Garden City, N.Y., 1965.†

2164 CLAGHORN, Kate Hollady. *The Immigrant's Day in Court.* New York, 1923.

2165 COBEN, Stanley. *A. Mitchell Palmer.* See **98.**

2166 COBEN, Stanley. "A Study in Nativism: The American Red Scare of 1919–1920." See **717.**

2167 CURTI, Merle E. *The Roots of American Loyalty.* See **729.**

2168 DANIELS, Roger. *The Politics of Prejudice.* See **1108.**

2169 FAIRCHILD, Henry P. "The Literacy Test and Its Making." See **1766.**

2170 GARIS, Roy. *Immigration Restriction.* See **1768.**

2171 GOSSETT, Thomas F. *Race: The History of an Idea in America.* Dallas, 1963.

2172 HANDLIN, Oscar. "American Views of the Jew at the Opening of the Twentieth Century." See **1772.**

2173 HANDLIN, Oscar. *Race and Nationality in American Life.* See **1773.**

2174 HANSEN, Marcus L. *The Immigrant in American History.* See **1775.**

2175 HARTMANN, Edward G. *The Movement to Americanize the Immigrant.* New York, 1948.

2176 HIGHAM, John. *Strangers in the Land.* See **53.**

2177 ICHIHASHI, Yamato. *Japanese in the United States.* See **1781.**

2178 JACKSON, Kenneth T. *The Ku Klux Klan in the City, 1915–1930.* New York, 1967.†

2179 JAFFE, Julian F. *Crusade Against Radicalism.* See **747.**

2180 JENKS, Jeremiah W., and W. Jett LAUCK. *The Immigrant Problem.* See **1782.**

2181 JENSEN, Joan M. *The Price of Vigilance.* See **1301.**

2182 JOHNSON, Donald D. *The Challenge to American Freedoms.* See **748.**

2183 KINZER, Donald E. *An Episode in Anti-Catholicism: The American Protective Association.* Seattle, 1964.

2184 KOHLER, Max. *Immigration and Aliens in the United States.* New York, 1936.

2185 LORENCE, James J. "Business and Reform: The American Asiatic Association and the Exclusion Laws, 1905–1907." *Pac Hist Rev,* XXXXIX (1970), 421–38.

2186 LOUCKS, Emerson H. *The Ku Klux Klan in Pennsylvania: A Study in Nativism.* Harrisburg, Pa., 1936.

2187 MATTHEWS, Fred H. "White Community and 'Yellow Peril.' " See **1789.**

2188 MC WILLIAMS, Carey. *A Mask for Privilege: Anti-Semitism in America.* Boston, 1948.

2189 MECKLIN, John M. *The Ku Klux Klan: A Study of the American Mind.* New York, 1924.

2190 MILLER, Robert M. "A Note of the Relationship between the Protestant Churches and the Ku Klux Klan." *J S Hist,* XXII (1956), 257–66.

2191 MILLIS, Harry A. *The Japanese Problem in the United States.* See **1792.**

2192 MURPHY, John C. *An Analysis of the Attitudes of American Catholics Toward the Immigrant and the Negro, 1825–1925.* Washington, D.C., 1940.

2193 MURRAY, Robert K. *Red Scare.* See **767.**

2194 MYERS, Gustavus. *A History of Bigotry in the United States.* New York, 1943.

2195 PRESTON, William, Jr. *Aliens and Dissenters.* See **779.**

2196 RICE, Arnold S. *The Ku Klux Klan in American Politics.* Washington, D.C., 1962.

2197 ROSS, Edward A. *Seventy Years of It.* See **204.**

2198 SANDMEYER, Elmer C. *The Anti-Chinese Movement in California.* See **1145.**

2199 SAVETH, Edward A. *American Historians and European Immigrants, 1875–1925.* New York, 1948.

2200 SCHEIBER, Harry N. *The Wilson Administration and Civil Liberties, 1917–1921.* See **781.**

2201 STAUFFER, Alvin P., Jr. "Anti-Catholicism in American Politics, 1865–1900." Doctoral dissertation, Harvard University, 1931.

2202 SWISHER, Carl B. "Civil Liberties in War Time." See **787.**

2203 TANNENBAUM, Frank. *Darker Phases of the South.* New York, 1924.

2204 TAYLOR, Joseph H. "The Restriction of European Immigration, 1890–1924." See **1801**.

2205 WARTH, Robert D. "The Palmer Raids." See **798**.

2206 WEAVER, Norman F. "The Knights of the Ku Klux Klan in Wisconsin, Indiana, Ohio, and Michigan." Doctoral dissertation, University of Wisconsin, 1954.

2207 WITTKE, Carl. *The German–Americans and the World War.* See **806**.

2208 WITTKE, Carl. *We Who Built America.* See **1808**.

10. Women

2209 ADDAMS, Jane. *The Second Twenty Years at Hull–House.* See **75**.

2210 ADDAMS, Jane. *Twenty Years at Hull–House.* See **76**.

2211 ATHEY, Louis L. "Florence Kelley and the Quest for Negro Equality." See **382**.

2212 BANNER, Lois W. *Women in Modern America: A Brief History.* New York, 1974.†

2213 BLUMBERG, Dorothy R. *Florence Kelley.* See **88**.

2214 BRECKINRIDGE, Sophonisba. *Women in the Twentieth Century.* See **1815**.

2215 BURNHAM, John C. "The Progressive Era Revolution in American Attitudes Toward Sex." See **1817**.

2216 BUSBEY, Katherine G. *Home Life in America.* See **1818**.

2217 CONWAY, Jill. "Women Reformers and American Culture, 1870–1930." *Journal of Social History,* V (1971–1972), 164–77.

2218 DAVIS, Allen F. *American Heroine.* See **111**.

2219 FETHERLING, Dale. *Mother Jones.* See **1659**.

2220 FLEXNER, Eleanor. *Century of Struggle.* See **250**.

2221 FULLER, Paul E. *Laura Clay and the Woman's Rights Movement.* Lexington, Ky., 1975.

2222 GOLDMARK, Josephine C. *Impatient Crusader.* See **126**.

2223 HALL, Frederick S., and Elisabeth W. BROOKE. *American Marriage Laws.* See **1820**.

2224 HILL, Joseph A. *Women in Gainful Occupations, 1870–1920.* See **1676**.

2225 JAMES, Edward T., *et al.,* eds. *Notable American Women, 1607–1950: A Biographical Dictionary.* 3 vols. Cambridge, Mass., 1971.

2226 KENNEALLY, James J. "Women and Trade Unions, 1870–1920: The Quandary of the Reformer." See **1684**.

2227 KENNEDY, David M. *Birth Control in America: The Career of Margaret Sanger.* New Haven, 1970.†

2228 KRADITOR, Aileen S. *The Ideas of the Woman Suffrage Movement, 1890–1920.* See **264**.

2229 LERNER, Gerda. *The Woman in American History.* Menlo Park, Cal., 1971.†

2230 LEVINE, Daniel. "Jane Addams: Romantic Radical, 1889–1912." See **407**.

2231 LEVINE, Daniel. *Jane Addams and the Liberal Tradition.* See **408.**

2232 LINN, James W. *Jane Addams.* See **174.**

2233 LUBOVE, Roy. "The Progressive and the Prostitute." See **412.**

2234 MC GOVERN, James R. "The American Woman's Pre-World War I Freedom in Manners and Morals." See **1826.**

2235 MORGAN, David. *Suffragists and Democrats: The Politics of Woman Suffrage in America.* East Lansing, Mich., 1972.

2236 O'NEILL, William L. *Divorce in the Progressive Era.* See **1829.**

2237 O'NEILL, William L. "Divorce in the Progressive Era." See **1830.**

2238 O'NEILL, William L. *Everyone Was Brave.* See **1831.**

2239 PAULSON, Ross E. *Women's Suffrage and Prohibition: A Comparative Study of Equality and Social Control.* Glenview, Ill., 1973.

2240 SCHAFFER, Ronald. "The Problem of Consciousness in the Woman Suffrage Movement: A California Perspective." *Pac Hist Rev,* XLV (1976), 469–94.

2241 SMUTS, Robert W. *Women and Work in America.* See **1834.**

2242 SOCHEN, June. *Movers and Shakers: American Women Thinkers and Activists, 1900–1970.* New York, 1973.†

2243 SOCHEN, June. *The New Woman: Feminism in Greenwich Village, 1910–1920.* New York, 1972.†

2244 STEEL, Edward M. "Mother Jones in the Fairmont Field, 1902." See **1725.**

2245 STEELMAN, Lala C. "Mary Clare de Graffenried: The Saga of a Crusader for Social Reform." See **418.**

2246 STIGLER, George J. *Domestic Servants in the United States, 1900–1940.* See **1835.**

2247 STROM, Sharon Hartman. "Leadership and Tactics in the American Woman Suffrage Movement: A New Perspective from Massachusetts." *J Am Hist,* LXII (1975), 296–315.

2248 TAYLOR, A. Elizabeth. *The Woman Suffrage Movement in Tennessee.* See **366.**

2249 WALD, Lillian. *The House of Henry Street.* See **224.**

INDEX

Aaron, Daniel, 486, 1837
Abell, Aaron I., 427, 428, 1939, 1940, 1941
Abrahams, Paul P., 1251
Abrams, Ray H., 695, 1938
Abrams, Richard M., 280, 281, 646
Adamic, Louis, 1625, 1749, 1750
Adams, Graham, Jr., 512, 1626
Adams, Henry, 1838
Addams, Jane, 75, 76, 379, 380, 2209, 2210
Adler, Selig, 696, 871, 985
Agg, Thomas R., 1542
Ahlstrom, Sydney E., 1942
Aiken, John R., 429, 1627
Aitken, Hugh G. T., 1487
Alexander, Charles C., 2156
Allen, Frederick Lewis, 1380, 1462, 1463
Allen, H. C., 1051
Allen, Howard W., 234, 235, 1165, 2086
Allport, Gordon W., 2157
Allswang, John M., 1751
Ambrosius, Lloyd E., 1252
Ameringer, Charles D., 986, 987
Anderson, Donald F., 513
Anderson, Eugene N., 1052
Anderson, H. Dewey, 1628
Anderson, Oscar E., Jr., 514
Andreano, Ralph, 1488
Andrews, John B., 1489
Aptheker, Herbert, 77, 2069
Armstrong, Maurice W., 1943
Arnett, Alex M., 697
Asher, Robert, 381
Atherton, Lewis E., 1810
Athey, Louis L., 382, 2070, 2211
Auerbach, Jerold S., 487
Auxier, George W., 920
Avin, Benjamin H., 2158

Baber, Ray E., 1811
Babcock, Kendric C., 1752
Babson, Roger W., 586, 1629
Bacon, Charles Reade, 282
Bagby, Wesley M., 698
Baigell, Matthew, 1986
Bailey, Hugh C., 78, 283
Bailey, Joseph C., 1583

Bailey, Kenneth K., 1944
Bailey, Liberty Hyde, 1584
Bailey, Thomas A., 872, 873, 874, 921, 1089, 1090, 1091, 1092, 1106, 1107, 1108, 1109, 1253, 1254, 1255
Baker, George, 988
Baker, John D., 515
Baker, O. E., 1398
Baker, Ray Stannard, 79, 80, 81, 587, 588, 1170, 1256, 2027
Banner, Lois W., 2212
Bannister, Robert C., Jr., 82, 2028
Barbeau, Arthur E., 699, 2071
Barbour, Jeffrey, 1418
Barfield, Claude E., 516
Barger, Harold, 1585
Baritz, Loren, 1490
Barker, Charles A., 83, 1839
Barker, John Marshall, 430, 1945
Barker, Virgil, 1987
Barnard, John, 431, 1872, 1946
Barr, Alwyn, 284
Barry, Coleman J., 1753, 1947
Bartlett, Ruhl J., 1257
Baruch, Bernard M., 700
Bassett, T. D. Seymour, 3
Bates, J. Leonard, 461, 462, 647
Baumgartner, Apollinaris W., 2029
Beale, Howard K., 875, 989, 1053, 1093
Bean, Walton E., 285
Beardsley, Edward H., 383
Beasley, Norman, 210, 684
Beaver, Daniel R., 701, 702
Beck, Holmes, 1873
Bedford, Henry F., 837
Beers, Burton F., 1094, 1095
Beisner, Robert L., 922
Bell, Herbert C. F., 84, 589
Bemis, Samuel Flagg, 4, 876, 990
Benedict, Murray R., 1586
Benison, Saul, 1914
Berbusse, Edward J., 991
Berger, Harold, 1491
Berglund, Abraham, 1492
Berle, Adolf A., 1414
Berman, Edward, 1630, 1631
Bernard, William S., 1754
Bernstein, Barton J., 923
Bernstorff, Johann H. von, 1171
Berry, Mary F., 2072, 2073

93

INDEX

Berthoff, Rowland T., 1755, 1756, 2159
Best, Gary D., 703, 704, 1632
Beth, Loren P., 808
Bethmann Hollweg, Theobald von, 1172
Bidwell, Percy W., 792
Billington, Monroe Lee, 85, 1173
Billington, Ray Allen, 1874, 1875
Bing, Alexander M., 705, 1633
Birdsall, Paul, 1174, 1258
Birnbaum, Karl E., 1175
Birr, Kendall, 1764
Blackford, Mansel G., 286, 1415
Blair, John M., 1616
Blaisdell, Thomas C., Jr., 35, 1416
Blake, Nelson M., 877
Blakey, George T., 706
Bleyer, Willard G., 2030
Blum, John M., 86, 87, 186, 517, 558, 590, 591, 592, 707, 960, 1026, 1133, 2160
Blumberg, Dorothy Rose, 88, 384, 2213
Blumenthal, Henry, 648, 2074
Bode, Frederick A., 1948
Bogan, Louise, 1988
Bogart, Ernest L., 708
Bogue, Allan G., 1587
Bonbright, James C., 1417, 1543
Boorstin, Daniel J., 1812
Boudin, Louis B., 809
Bourke, Paul F., 488, 1840, 1841
Bowden, Henry W., 1949
Bowers, Claude G., 89, 236
Bowers, David F., 1757, 2161
Bowers, William L., 1813, 1814
Boyd, Betty, 1758
Braeman, John, 90, 237, 518, 519
Bragdon, Henry W., 91, 593
Braisted, William R., 1096, 1097, 1098, 1099
Brandeis, Elizabeth, 36, 1634
Brandeis, Louis D., 1464
Brandes, Stuart D., 1381
Brauer, Jerald C., 1950
Breckenridge, Sophonisba, 1815, 2214
Bremner, Robert H., 385, 386, 387, 1816
Brindley, John E., 1542
Brissenden, Paul F., 838, 1635, 1636
Britt, George, 2031
Broderick, Francis L., 92, 2075
Brody, David, 709, 1637, 1638
Broesamle, John J., 93, 594, 649, 1465
Brooke, Elisabeth W., 1820, 2223

Brooks, Aubrey L., 94, 238
Brooks, Van Wyck, 1989, 1990
Brown, Charles H., 2032
Brown, Dorothy M., 2033
Bruno, Frank Jr., 388
Bryan, Mary B., 95, 239, 1176
Bryant, Keith L., Jr., 389, 1639
Buchanan, Russell, 1177
Buckler, Helen, 1915, 2076
Buder, Stanley, 1640
Buehrig, Edward H., 1178, 1179, 1259
Buell, Raymond L., 1100
Buenker, John D., 240, 241, 287, 288
Buley, R. Carlyle, 1493
Bullock, Charles T., 878
Buni, Andrew, 2077
Bunting, David, 1418
Burbank, Garin, 1588
Burdick, Frank, 650
Burner, David, 595, 651, 710
Burnett, Philip M., 1260
Burnham, John C., 1817, 1916, 2215
Burns, Arthur R., 1419, 1420
Burns, Edward M., 1876
Buroker, Robert L., 1759
Burr, Nelson R., 6
Burton, David H., 520, 521, 924, 925, 1054, 1055
Burts, Robert M., 289
Busbey, Katherine G., 1818, 2216
Butler, Nicholas Murray, 1877
Butt, Archibald W., 96, 522
Butts, R. Freeman, 1878

Caine, Stanley P., 290, 291, 1544
Callcott, Margaret L., 2078
Callcott, Wilfrid A., 992
Calvert, Peter, 993
Cambon, Henri, 1180
Cameron, Meribeth E., 1101
Campbell, Alexander E., 1056
Campbell, Charles S., Jr., 1057
Campbell, E. G., 1545
Campbell, John P., 1058
Cargill, Oscar, 1842
Carosso, Vincent, 1466
Carpenter, Niles, 1760
Carstensen, Vernon, 1884
Catton, William B., 61
Chafee, Zechariah, Jr., 711, 2162
Challener, Richard D., 879
Chalmers, David M., 2163
Chamberlain, John, 37, 242

94

INDEX

Chambers, Clarke A., 390
Chambers, David M., 443
Chaney, Lucian W., 1494
Chapin, Robert C., 1641
Chase, Gilbert, 1991
Chatfield, Charles, 712
Chay, Jongsuk, 1102
Chessman, G. Wallace, 97, 523
Child, Clifton J., 1181, 1761
Chrislock, Carl H., 292
Chudacoff, Howard P., 1399, 1762
Churchill, Winston S., 1182, 1261
Claghorn, Kate Hollady, 2164
Clapesattle, Helen, 1917
Clark, Earle, 1400
Clark, John Bates, 38, 1421
Clark, John D., 39, 652, 1422
Clark, John Maurice, 38, 714, 1421
Clark, Victor S., 1495
Clark, Walter E., 1437
Clarkson, Grosvenor B., 715
Clausen, Aage R., 2068
Clay, Howard B., 524
Clemen, Rudolf A., 1496
Clendenen, Clarence C., 994
Clews, Henry, 1467
Clifford, John G., 596
Clinard, Outten J., 1103
Cline, Howard F., 995
Clubb, Jerome M., 235, 2068
Clymer, Kenton J., 926
Coben, Stanley, 98, 716, 717, 1382,
   2165, 2166
Cochran, Negley D., 2034
Cochran, Thomas C., 1383, 1384, 1497
Coffman, Edward M., 718, 1262
Cohen, Naomi W., 99, 525, 1059
Coit, Margaret L., 100, 719
Coker, William S., 1060
Cole, Arthur H., 1498
Coletta, Paola E., 101, 243, 526, 880,
   927, 928, 996, 1104
Commager, Henry S., 489, 1843
Commons, John R., 102, 1763
Condit, Carl W., 1992, 1993, 1994
Conlin, Joseph R., 839, 840, 841, 1642,
   1643, 2035
Conway, Jill, 2217
Coombs, Whitney, 1644
Cooper, John M., Jr., 881, 1183
Copeland, Melvin T., 1499
Copley, Frank B., 1500
Corey, Lewis, 1468
Cornell, Robert J., 527

Corwin, Edward S., 810, 811, 812
Cosmas, Graham A., 929
Costrell, Edwin, 720
Cramer, Clarence H., 103, 721, 1263
Creel, George, 104, 1264, 2036
Cremin, Lawrence A., 1878, 1879
Crighton, John C., 722, 1184
Croly, Herbert D., 105, 528, 1105
Cronin, Barnard C., 1645
Cronon, E. David, 106, 597, 598, 1185,
   1265
Crooks, James B., 293
Cross, Whitney R., 463
Crow, Jeffrey J., 294
Crowe, Charles, 2080
Crowell, Benedict, 723
Crunden, Robert M., 107, 444
Cubberly, Ellwood P., 1880, 1881
Cuddy, Edward, 1186, 1951
Cuff, Robert D., 724, 725, 726, 727
Culshaw, John, 1995
Cumberland, Charles C., 997
Cummins, Cedric C., 728
Current, Richard N., 1266
Currie, Harold W., 842
Curry, George, 1267
Curry, Roy W., 1106, 1107
Curti, Merle E., 490, 729, 1187, 1764,
   1844, 1882, 1883, 1884, 2167
Cushman, Robert E., 40, 1423
Cutlip, Scott M., 244
Cywar, Alan, 491, 492, 730, 1845

Dabney, Charles W., 1885
Dabney, Thomas E., 2037
Daniel, Pete, 2081
Daniel, Robert L., 1061
Daniels, George H., 1918
Daniels, Josephus, 108, 109, 110, 245,
   246, 599, 1188, 1268, 2038, 2039
Daniels, Roger, 1108, 1765, 2168
Dankof, Ralph H., 1516
Darling, Arthur B., 464
Davidson, Elizabeth H., 392, 1646
Davidson, John Wells, 600, 653
Davidson, Percy E., 1628
Davies, George R., 1402
Davis, Allen F., 111, 393, 394, 395,
   396, 731, 2218
Davis, Calvin D., 1062, 1063
Davis, G. Cullom, 654
Davis, George T., 882
Day, Edmund E., 1501

INDEX

Dearing, Charles L., 1546
De Jouvenel, Bertrand, 601
De Kruif, Paul, 1919
Dennett, Tyler, 930, 1064, 1109, 1110
Dennis, A. L. P., 931, 998, 1065, 1111
De Novo, John A., 883
Derber, Milton, 397, 1647
Deutsch, Albert, 1920
Devlin, Patrick, 1189
De Weerd, Harvey A., 1270
Dewing, Arthur S., 1424, 1469
De Witt, Benjamin Parke, 247
Dexter, Byron, 7
Diamond, Sigmund, 1385
Diamond, William, 602
Dick, William M., 843, 1648
Dietel, Else H., 1661
Dignan, Don K., 1271
Dimock, Marshall E., 603
Dingman, Roger, 884
Director, Aaron, 1651
Dixon, Frank H., 1547
Dodd, William E., 81, 588
Dodds, Gordon B., 465, 1607
Doerries, Reinhard R., 1190
Doezema, William R., 1425, 1548
Doherty, Herbert J., Jr., 295
Donahue, Gilbert E., 31
Dorfman, Joseph, 493, 494, 1846, 1847
Dorn, Jacob H., 432, 1952
Dorsett, Lyle W., 41
Doster, James F., 1549
Douglas, Paul H., 1649, 1650, 1651
Dowing, Cedric B., 1470
Downer, Alan S., 1996
Draper, Theodore, 732
Dubin, Martin D., 1191
Dubofsky, Melvyn, 296, 844, 845, 1652, 1653, 1654
Dudden, Arthur P., 1848
Duff, John B., 1272
Dulles, Foster Rhea, 885, 932, 1819
Dunne, Gerald T., 813
Dupree, A. Hunter, 1921, 1922
Duroselle, Jean Baptiste, 886, 906
Durrand, Edward D., 1426
Dykhuizen, George, 1849

Eastman, Crystal, 398, 1655
Eaton, Leonard K., 1997
Eddy, Arthur J., 1427
Edmonds, Helen G., 2082
Edwards, George W., 1471

Egbert, Donald D., 846
Eichner, Alfred S., 1428
Eighmy, John L., 1953
Ekirch, Arthur A., Jr., 1850
Ellis, Elmer, 112, 2040
Ellis, John Tracy, 8, 1954, 1955
Ellis, L. Ethan, 887
Ely, Richard T., 113, 248
Ensley, Philip C., 733, 1656
Epstein, Klaus, 1192, 1273
Epstein, Ralph C., 1608
Ershkowitz, Herbert, 888
Esthus, Raymond A., 889, 1112, 1113, 1114
Eyre, James E., Jr., 933

Fabela, Isidro, 999
Fabricant, Solomon, 1502, 1657
Fainsod, Merle, 42, 1429
Fairchild, Henry P., 1766, 2169
Farrell, John C., 1851
Farrell, John T., 934
Faulkner, Harold U., 43, 44, 1386, 1658
Fausold, Martin L., 114, 604
Felt, Jeremy P., 399
Ferguson, Maxwell, 1550
Ferrell, Henry C., Jr., 297
Ferrell, Robert H., 605, 1274
Fetherling, Dale, 1659, 2219
Fifield, Russell H., 1115
Fike, Claude E., 1275, 1276
Filene, Peter G., 249, 890
Filler, Louis, 9, 445, 446, 447
Fine, Sidney, 45
Fink, Gary M., 10, 1660
Finkelstein, Maurice, 814
Fischer, Fritz, 1193, 1277
Fish, John O., 1956, 2083
Fisher, Mary, 22
Fitch, James M., 1998
Fite, Gilbert C., 476, 778
Fitzgibbon, Russell H., 1000
Flannagan, John H. Jr., 1278
Fleming, Denna F., 1194, 1279
Fleming, Donald, 1923
Flexner, Eleanor, 250, 2220
Flexner, J. T., 1924
Flexner, Simon, 1924
Flink, James J., 1551
Flinn, Alfred D., 1609
Flint, Winston Allen, 298
Floto, Inga, 1280

INDEX

Flynt, Wayne, 115, 299
Foerster, Robert F., 1661, 1767
Foner, Philip S., 935, 1662
Forcey, Charles, 495
Ford, Worthington D., 1852
Fosdick, Raymond B., 1281
Fowler, Dorothy, 116, 529
Fowler, Wilton B., 1282
Fox, Daniel M., 496, 1853
Fox, Richard W., 847
Fox, Stephen R., 2084
Fraenkel, Ernst, 906
Frankfurter, Felix, 815, 1663
Franklin, John Hope, 46, 2085
Frazier, E. Franklin, 2086
Freidel, Frank, 11, 117, 606, 936, 937, 1283
French, Carroll E., 1664
French, John C., 1886
Friedman, Milton, 1387
Frost, Richard H., 1665
Frothingham, Thomas G., 1284
Fry, Michael G., 1285
Fuller, Joseph V., 1001, 1116, 1195
Fuller, Paul E., 2221
Furniss, Norman F., 1957

Gabriel, Ralph, H., 497, 1854
Galambos, Louis, 1430, 1589, 1666, 1667
Galishoff, Stuart, 1925
Galpin, Charles J., 1401
Garis, Roy L., 1768, 2170
Garraty, John A., 118, 119, 120, 121, 530, 607, 608, 609, 816, 1286, 1472, 1503, 1667
Gaskill, Nelson B., 1431
Gates, John M., 938
Gatewood, Willard B., Jr., 531, 532, 939, 940, 2087, 2088
Gaus, John M., 1590
Gaustad, Edwin S., 1958
Geiger, Louis G., 122, 300
Geismar, Maxwell D., 1999, 2000
Gelber, Lionel M., 1066
Gelfand, Lawrence E., 1287
Genthe, Charles V., 734
George, Alexander L., 123, 610
George, Juliette L., 123, 610
Gerard, James W., 1196
German, James C., Jr., 533, 534, 1432
Gerson, Louis L., 1288
Geselbracht, Raymond H., 2001

Gibb, George Sweet, 1504
Gilbert, Charles, 735
Gilbert, James, 1855
Gillette, Howard, Jr., 1002
Gillette, John M., 1402
Ginger, Ray, 47, 124, 848
Gini, Corrado, 1403
Gist, Genevieve B., 301
Glaab, Charles N., 302
Glad, Paul W., 125, 251
Glass, Carter, 655, 1473
Glazer, Nathan, 1959
Glicksberg, Charles E., 2002
Gluck, Elsie, 1668
Godfrey, Aaron A., 736
Goedecke, Robert, 817
Goldenweiser, Emanuel A., 1591
Goldman, Eric F., 498, 737
Goldmark, Josephine C., 126, 400, 2222
Goldsmith, Raymond W., 1388
Gompers, Samuel, 127, 1669
Goodhart, C. A. E., 1474
Goodrich, Carter, 1404
Gordon, Lincoln, 42, 1429
Gordon, Milton M., 1769
Gossett, Thomas F., 2171
Gottfried, Alex, 128, 303
Gottschalk, Stephen, 1960
Gould, Lewis L., 252, 304
Graebner, Norman A., 891
Graham, Otis L., Jr., 253
Grantham, Dewey W., Jr., 12, 129, 254, 305, 656, 1289
Graves, William S., 1290
Graybar, Lloyd J., 130, 1856, 2041
Grayson, Cary T., 131, 611
Green, Constance, 306
Green, Fletcher M., 307
Green, Marguerite, 48, 1670
Greenbaum, Fred, 132, 308
Greene, Fred, 892
Greene, Lorenzo J., 2089
Greene, N., 1663
Greene, Victor, 1770
Greenlee, Howard S., 612
Greer, Thomas H., 401
Gregory, Charles O., 1671
Gregory, Horace, 2003
Gregory, Ross, 133, 1197, 1198, 1199
Grenville, John A. S., 893
Grew, Joseph C., 1200, 1291
Grey, Edward (Viscount Grey of Fallodon), 1201
Grieb, Kenneth J., 1003

INDEX

Griffin, Grace Gardner, 4
Griffith, Ernest S., 309
Griffith, Kathryn, 49
Griffith, Linda A., 2004
Griswold, A. Whitney, 1117
Grubbs, Frank L., Jr., 1672
Gruber, Carol S., 738, 1887
Grunder, Garel A., 1118
Gulick, Charles A., 66, 682, 1455, 1482
Gustin, Laurence R., 1552
Gutteridge, Leonard F., 675
Gwynn, Stephen, 1067, 1202, 1292
Gwinn, William Rea, 134, 535

Haber, Samuel, 255, 1505
Hackney, Sheldon, 310
Hagedorn, Hermann, 135, 136, 536,
    739, 1004, 1203, 1204
Hale, Nathan G., Jr., 1926
Haley, P. Edward, 1005
Hall, Frederick S., 1820, 2223
Hall, Luella J., 1068
Hall, Tom G., 740, 1592
Hamilton, Walton H., 818, 1433, 1610
Hammond, John W., 1506
Handlin, Oscar, 1771, 1772, 1773, 1774,
    2172, 2173
Handy, Robert T., 849, 1961
Hanna, Hugh S., 1494
Hansen, Alvin H., 1673
Hansen, Marcus L., 1775, 1776, 2174
Harbaugh, William H., 137, 138, 537,
    941, 1006, 1069, 1119, 1205
Harbeson, Robert W., 50, 1553
Harbison, Winfred A., 820
Harbord, James G., 1293
Harding, T. Swann, 1593
Hargreaves, Mary Wilma M., 1594
Harlan, Louis R., 139, 140, 2090, 2091,
    2092, 2093, 2094
Harrington, Fred H., 942, 943, 1120
Harris, Abram L., 2139
Harris, Carl V., 2095
Harris, Leon, 141, 448, 2042
Harris, Seymour E., 657, 1475
Harrow, Benjamin, 1927
Hart, Robert A., 894
Hartmann, Edward G., 2175
Hartz, Louis, 499
Haughton, Virginia, 658, 1674
Hawkins, Hugh, 1888
Hays, Samuel P., 51, 52, 311, 466
Heald, Morrell, 1777

Healy, David F., 944, 1007, 1008
Heath, Frederick M., 312, 1675
Heaton, John L., 2043
Hechler, Kenneth W., 538
Heckscher, August, 613, 614
Heindel, Richard H., 1070
Heinrichs, Waldo H., Jr., 1206
Helbich, Wolfgang J., 1294
Helmes, Winifred G., 142, 313
Henderson, Gerard C., 1434
Hendrick, Burton J., 143, 144, 1207,
    1295, 1507
Hendrickson, Kenneth E., Jr., 741, 850
Henri, Florette, 699, 1405, 2071, 2096
Herberg, Will, 1962
Herbst, Jurgen, 1889
Herman, Sondra R., 895
Herring, George C., Jr., 1208
Hessen, Robert, 1508
Hewes, James E., 1296
Hicks, Granville, 230, 460, 2005, 2065
Hicks, John D., 482, 1599
Hidy, Muriel E., 1509
Hidy, Ralph W., 1509
Higgs, Robert, 1406, 1595, 2097
Higham, John, 13, 53, 1778, 2176
Hill, Forest G., 1382
Hill, Joseph A., 1676, 2224
Hill, Larry D., 1009
Hillje, John W., 256
Hillquit, Morris, 851
Himmelberg, Robert F., 742, 1435
Hindman, E. James, 896
Hines, Thomas S., 2006
Hines, Walker D., 743
Hirst, David W., 314, 1209
Hitchman, James H., 945
Hoffman, Frederick J., 2007
Hofstadter, Richard, 54, 257, 500, 946,
    1857, 1858
Hogan, Michael J., 1297
Hoglund, A. William, 1780
Hohman, Elmo P., 659, 1677, 1678
Holbo, Paul S., 1010
Holden, Arthur C., 402
Holl, Jack M., 403
Holley, I. B., Jr., 1611
Holli, Melvin G., 315
Hollingsworth, J. Rogers, 55, 539
Holmes, William F., 145, 540, 2098
Holt, James, 541, 615
Holt, W. Stull, 1298, 1890
Homer, William I., 2008
Hoogenboom, Ari, 1436, 1554

Hoogenboom, Olive, 1436, 1554
Hook, Sidney, 501, 1859, 1891
Hoover, Edgar M., Jr., 1407, 1510
Hoover, Herbert, 1299
Hopkins, C. Howard, 442
Hopkins, Charles H., 433, 1963, 1967
Hornig, Edgar A., 542
Houchins, Chang-su, 1779
Houchins, Lee, 1779
Houston, David F., 146, 616
Hovenstine, E. Jay, Jr., 744
Howard, John T., 2009, 2010
Howard, Leon, 2011
Howe, Frederic C., 147, 258, 404
Howe, M. A. DeWolfe, 148, 543
Hudson, James J., 1300
Hudson, Winthrop S., 1965
Hughes, Thomas P., 1612
Hunt, Michael H., 1121
Huntington–Wilson, F. M., 1122
Hurley, Edward N., 745
Hutchins, John G. B., 1555
Hutchinson, William T., 149, 617
Huthmacher, J. Joseph, 150, 316, 317

Ichihashi, Yamato, 1781, 2177
Iriye, Akira, 1123
Ise, John, 660, 1511
Israel, Fred L., 28
Israel, Jerry, 1124, 1125
Issac, Paul E., 318

Jack, Robert L., 259, 2099
Jackson, Kenneth T., 2178
Jaffe, Julian F., 747, 2179
James, Edward T., 2225
James, Marquis, 1512
Jamieson, Stuart, 477, 1596
Jamison, Alden, 1071
Jamison, A. Leland, 1979
Janick, Herbert, 319
Jeffreys–Jones, Rhodi, 1680
Jenks, Jeremiah Whipple, 1437, 1782, 2180
Jensen, Billie Barnes, 661, 1681
Jensen, Joan M., 1301, 2181
Jerome, Harry, 1408, 1613
Jessup, Philip C., 151, 544, 1011, 1072, 1126
Johnson, Allen, 14
Johnson, Arthur M., 545, 1438
Johnson, Carolyn W., 546

Johnson, Charles S., 2100
Johnson, Donald D., 748, 2182
Johnson, Emory R., 1389
Johnson, Guion Griffis, 2101
Johnson, Neil M., 1210
Johnson, Stanley C., 1783
Johnson, Tom L., 152, 320
Johnson, Walter, 153, 2044
Johnson, Warren B., 449
Jones, Eliot, 1439
Jones, Maldwyn Allen, 1784
Joost, Nicholas, 1860
Josephson, Matthew, 1614

Kahle, Louis G., 1012
Kandel, I. L., 1892
Kaplan, Justin, 154, 450, 2045
Kaplan, Louis, 15
Kaplan, Sidney, 749
Karraker, William A., 947
Karson, Marc, 56, 1682
Kaufman, Burton I., 897, 898, 899, 1013
Kazin, Alfred, 2012
Keir, Malcolm, 1513
Keller, Morton, 819, 1514
Kellogg, Charles Flint, 260, 2102
Kelly, Alfred H., 820
Kelly, Fred C., 1615
Kemble, John H., 1556
Kemmerer, Edwin W., 662
Kendrick, John W., 1390
Kennan, George, 1557
Kennan, George F., 900, 1302, 1303
Kenneally, James J., 1684, 2226
Kennedy, Albert J., 425
Kennedy, David M., 262, 2227
Kennedy, Edward D., 1558
Kennedy, Louise V., 1409, 2103, 2124
Kerney, James, 155, 618
Kerr, James J., IV, 663
Kerr, K. Austin, 750, 1515, 1559
Kerr, Thomas J., IV, 405
Kerr, William T., Jr., 321
Kessner, Thomas, 1785
Kester, Randall B., 751
Kevles, Daniel J., 752, 753, 754, 1928, 1929
Kihl, Mary R., 1304
King, Judson, 467
King, Willard L., 821
King, Willford I., 3191, 1392
Kinzer, Donald E., 2183

INDEX

Kipnis, Ira A., 852
Kirby, J. T., 2104
Kirsh, Benjamin S., 1440
Kirwan, Albert D., 322
Klebaner, Benjamin J., 664, 1441
Klein, Ira, 1305
Klinkhamer, Marie C., 822
Kluger, James R., 1685
Knauth, Oswald Whitman, 1442
Knight, Edgar W., 1893
Knoles, George H., 755
Knowlton, Evelyn H., 1504
Knox, Israel, 1966
Kohler, Max, 2184
Koistinen, Paul A. C., 756
Kolko, Gabriel, 57, 58, 263, 1560
Kousser, J. Morgan, 59
Kraditor, Aileen S., 264, 2228
Kube, Harold D., 1516
Kuehl, Warren F., 16, 901
Kuhlmann, Charles B., 1517
Kurland, Gerald, 156, 323
Kusmer, Kenneth L., 406
Kutler, Stanley I., 823, 1686
Kuznetz, Simon, 1476

Lafeber, Walter, 948
La Follette, Belle C., 157, 547, 619
La Follette, Fola, 157, 547, 619
La Forte, Robert S., 324
Lahne, Herbert J., 1687
Lambert, John R., 158
Lambert, Oscar D., 159, 548
Lancaster, James L., 1306
Landsberg, Hans H., 1585
Lane, Ann J., 549, 2105
Lane, Anne W., 160, 620
Lane, James B., 451
Lanfear, Vincent W., 1688
Langer, William L., 1211, 1307, 1308
Lankford, John E., 1967
Lansing, Robert, 1309, 1310
Larsen, Charles, 161, 325
Larsen, William, 162, 326
Larson, Bruce L., 163
Larson, Cedric, 763
Larson, Henrietta M., 17, 1518
Lasch, Christopher, 502, 949, 1311, 1312
Laslett, John H. M., 853, 1689
Lasswell, Harold D., 757
Latham, Earl, 621

Latimer, Murray W., 1690
Lauck, W. Jett, 1691, 1782, 2180
Laughlin, J. Laurence, 665, 1477
Layman, Martha E., 1223
Layton, Edwin T., Jr., 1930
Lazerson, Marvin, 1894
Leary, William M., Jr., 666
Lebow, Richard N., 1313
Lefler, Hugh T., 94, 238
Leiby, James, 1692
Leigh, Robert D., 1931
Leiserson, William M., 1786
Leopold, Richard W., 164, 550, 902, 903, 904, 1014, 1073, 1127, 1212
Lerner, Gerda, 2229
Lerner, Max, 824
Lescohier, Don D., 60, 1693, 1694
Leuchtenburg, William E., 950, 758
Levin, N. Gordon, Jr., 1314
Levine, Daniel, 165, 265, 407, 408, 1695, 2230, 2231
Levine, Lawrence W., 166, 759
Levy, David W., 220, 278, 641
Le Warne, Charles P., 1821
Lewis, Cleona, 905
Lieb, Franklin A., 923
Lieberman, Elias, 1696
Linderman, Gerald F., 951
Link, Arthur S., 19, 61, 167, 168, 169, 170, 171, 172, 173, 327, 551, 622, 623, 624, 625, 626, 627, 628, 629, 667, 668, 669, 670, 671, 672, 673, 906, 1015, 1016, 1017, 1018, 1019, 1129, 1213, 1214, 1215, 1216, 1217, 1315
Linkh, Richard M., 1787
Linn, James Weber, 174, 409, 2232
Li, Tien-yi, 1128
Livermore, Seward W., 760, 761, 1021, 1130
Livesay, Harold C., 1443
Livezey, William E., 907, 1118
Lloyd George, David, 1218, 1316
Locklin, D. Philip, 1516
Lockmiller, David A., 1022
Logan, Rayford W., 1317, 2106
Lombardi, John, 1697
Loos, John L., 1519
Lord, Walter, 1822
Lorence, James J., 2185
Lorwin, Lewis L., 1616, 1698
Lou, Herbert H., 1823
Loucks, Emerson H., 2186

Louis, William R., 1318
Lower, Richard C., 1319
Lowitt, Richard, 175, 176, 328, 468, 552, 630, 1219, 1562
Lowry, Bullitt, 1320
Lubove, Roy, 410, 411, 412, 413, 414, 415, 2233
Luebke, Frederick C., 762, 1788
Lyon, Peter, 452, 2046
Lytle, Richard H., 1617

McAdoo, William G., 182, 631
McAvoy, Thomas T., 1970, 1971
McClellan, Robert, 1790
McCloskey, Robert G., 1864
McCormick, Thomas J., 955, 1131
McDonald, Forrest, 1521, 1522
McDonnell, James R., 429, 1627
McFarland, Marvin W., 1618
McGann, Thomas F., 1023
McGeary, M. Nelson, 183, 469, 554
McGovern, George S., 674, 675
McGovern, James R., 1826, 2234
McKee, Delber L., 956
McKee, John D., 184, 2947
McKelvey, Blake, 333
McLaughlin, Glen E., 1523
McLaurin, Melton A., 1702
McPherson, James M., 21, 1895, 2108, 2109, 2110
McReynolds, George E., 1153
McWilliams, Carey, 2188
Madison, Charles A., 266
Malone, Dumas, 14
Mamatey, Victor S., 1321
Mandell, Bernard, 177, 1699, 1700, 2107
Mane, Robert, 1861
Mangold, George B., 1824
Mann, Arthur, 178, 329, 503
Manny, Theodore B., 1401
Mantoux, Paul, 1322
Marcell, David W., 1862
Marchand, C. Roland, 267
Margulies, Herbert F., 330
Martin, Abro, 179, 268, 1563, 1564
Martin, Laurence W., 1323, 1324
Mason, Alpheus T., 180, 269, 358, 504, 553, 825, 1578, 1701
Mason, Edward S., 1565
Matthews, Fred H., 1789, 2187
Matthews, Marcia M., 2014
Maxwell, Kenneth R., 1325

Maxwell, Robert S., 181, 331, 332
May, Ernest R., 20, 952, 953, 954, 1220, 1221
May, George S., 1520, 1566
May, Henry F., 434, 1825, 1863, 1968
Mayer, Arno J., 1326, 1327
Maynard, Theodore, 1969
Mead, Edward Sherwood, 1444
Means, Gardiner C., 1414, 1417
Mecklin, John M., 2189
Meier, August, 2111, 2112, 2113, 2114, 2115
Meier, Heinz K., 1074
Merrill, Horace S., 555
Merrill, Marion G., 555
Merritt, Richard L., 1328
Mervin, David, 1329
Meyer, Balthasar Henry, 556, 1445
Miller, David Hunter, 1330
Miller, Elizabeth W., 22
Miller, Herbert H., 1791, 1795
Miller, Robert Moats, 435, 1972, 2190
Miller, Sally M., 854, 855, 856, 2116
Miller, Sidney L., 1567
Miller, William D., 334, 1384
Miller, Zane L., 335
Millett, Allan R., 1024
Millis, Harry A., 1792, 2191
Millis, Walter, 1222
Mills, Frederick C., 62, 1446
Mims, Edwin, 1896
Minger, Ralph E., 908, 1025, 1132
Mitchell, Wesley C., 63, 1393, 1447
Mock, James R., 763, 764
Moger, Allen W., 336
Moline, Norman T., 1827
Moody, John, 1448, 1478
Mooney, Chase C., 1223
Moore, Charles W., 1524
Moore, Ernest C., 1897
Moore, R. Laurence, 857, 858, 2117
More, Louise B., 1703
Morgan, David, 2235
Morgan, H. Wayne, 859, 860, 957, 958, 959
Morison, Elting E., 185, 186, 557, 558, 960, 1026, 1133, 1331, 1619
Morison, Samuel E., 1898
Morlan, Robert L., 478
Morris, Lloyd R., 1828
Morris, Richard B., 23
Morris, Stuart, 270
Morrison, Joseph L., 2048
Morrissey, Alice, 1224

INDEX

Mott, Frank L., 453, 454, 2049, 2050
Mott, Rodney L., 826
Mott, T. Bentley, 1332
Moulton, Harold G., 1449, 1568, 1569
Mowry, George E., 24, 337, 338, 559, 560
Moynihan, James H., 1973
Mullendorf, William C., 765
Muller, Dorothea R., 436
Munro, Dana G., 1027, 1028, 1029
Murphy, John C., 2192
Murphy, Paul L., 632
Murray, Robert K., 676, 766, 767, 1704, 2193
Myers, Gustavus, 2194
Myers, Margaret G., 1479
Myrdal, Gunnar, 2118

Nadworthy, Milton J., 1705
Nash, Gerald D., 768, 1525, 1706
Neal, Larry, 1451
Neale, R. G., 961
Nelli, Humbert S., 339, 1793
Nelson, Clifford L., 1794
Nelson, Daniel, 1526, 1527, 1707, 1708
Nelson, Keith L., 1333
Nelson, Milton Nels, 1452
Nethers, John L., 1899
Neu, Charles E., 1134, 1135
Neufield, Maurice F., 26
Nevins, Allan, 187, 1075, 1528, 1570, 2051
Newby, I. A., 769, 2119, 2120
Newcomer, Mabel, 1529
Nicholas, Herbert G., 633, 906
Nicolson, Harold, 1334
Noble, David W., 505, 2052
Noble, Ransom E., Jr., 340
Noble, Stuart G., 1900
Noggle, Burl, 770
Norris, George W., 188, 341
Notter, Harley, 1225
Nourse, Edwin G., 1597
Noyes, Alexander D., 771, 1480, 1481
Nye, Russel B., 342

O'Brien, Francis W., 189, 772, 1335
O'Connor, Harvey, 1530
O'Connor, William V., 2015
Odegard, Peter H., 271
O'Gara, Gordon C., 561
O'Grady, Joseph P., 1336

Olcott, Charles S., 962
Older, Fremont, 190, 2053
Olin, Spencer C., Jr., 343
Oliver, John W., 1620
Olmstead, Clifton E., 1974
O'Neill, William L., 1829, 1830, 1831, 2236, 2237, 2238
Orr, Oliver H., Jr., 191, 344
Osborn, George C., 192, 193, 345
Osburn, W. J., 1901
Osgood, Robert E., 909, 1337
Ostrander, Gilman M., 346

Palmer, Frederick, 194, 773, 1226, 1338, 1339
Park, Robert W., 1795
Parrini, Carl P., 1340
Patrick, Rembert W., 19
Patterson, Thomas G., 910
Paulson, Ross E., 2239
Paxson, Frederic L., 634, 774, 775, 776
Peffer, E. Louise, 470
Pelling, Henry, 1709
Penick, James, Jr., 471, 562
Perkins, Bradford, 1076
Perkins, Dexter, 195, 677, 827, 1030, 1341
Perlman, Mark, 1710
Perlman, Selig, 64, 1711, 1712
Perry, Ralph Barton, 1865
Pershing, John J., 1342, 1343
Persons, Stow, 846
Peterson, Horace C., 778, 779
Peterson, Theodore, 2054
Phelps, William L., 2016
Pickens, Donald K., 506, 1866
Pierson, George W., 1902
Pike, Frederick B., 1031
Pinkett, Harold T., 196, 472, 563
Pitkin, William A., 564
Poincaré, Raymond, 1227, 1344
Porter, Eugene, 678
Porter, Kenneth W., 1518
Porter, Patrick G., 1443
Posey, John P., 1345
Potter, David M., 1832
Potts, E. Daniel, 347
Pratt, Julius W., 911, 963, 964, 965, 1032, 1136, 1228, 1346
Prescott, Francis C., 1137
Preston, William, Jr., 779, 2195
Pringle, Henry F., 197, 198, 565, 566, 1033, 1034, 1077, 1078, 1138, 1139

INDEX

Prisco, Salvatore, III, 912
Pruessen, Ronald W., 1347
Pugach, Noel, 1140
Puleston, William D., 966
Pulley, Raymond H., 348
Pusey, Merlo J., 199, 349, 679, 828
Pyle, Joseph G., 1571

Quandt, Jean B., 507, 1867
Quint, Howard H., 861, 967
Quirk, Robert E., 1035, 1036

Ragan, Fred D., 829
Rappaport, Armin, 1229
Ratner, Sidney, 65, 680, 1453
Raucher, Alan R., 1394
Rauschenbusch, Walter, 437, 438, 1975, 1976
Rayback, Joseph G., 1713
Read, James M., 1230
Redkey, Edwin S., 2121
Reed, Louis S., 1714
Rees, Albert, 1715
Regier, Cornelius C., 455
Reid, Ira DeA., 2122
Reinsch, Paul S., 1141
Remer, C. F., 1142
Reuter, Frank T., 968
Reynolds, George M., 350
Rice, Arnold S., 2196
Richardson, Elmo R., 473
Rideout, Walter B., 2017
Ringenbach, Paul T., 351, 416
Ripley, William Z., 567, 1572, 1573
Rippy, J. Fred, 1037, 1038
Ritter, Gerhard, 1231, 1348
Robbins, Roy M., 474
Roberts, Henry L., 27
Roberts, Mary M., 1932
Roche, John P., 830
Rodgers, Andrew D., III, 1933
Roelofs, Vernon W., 831
Roosevelt, Theodore, 200, 568, 1039, 1079, 1143
Roper, Daniel C., 202, 635
Roseberry, C. R., 1621
Rosenberg, Arnold S., 352
Rosenberg, Charles E., 1622
Rosenstone, Robert A., 203, 862
Ross, Barbara J., 2123
Ross, Edward A., 204, 417, 1811, 2197
Ross, Frank A., 2124

Rossi, Alice S., 1903
Rossi, Peter H., 1903
Rossiter, Frank R., 2018
Rossiter, William S., 1410
Rothstein, Morton, 1080
Rublee, George, 681
Rucker, Darnell, 1868
Rudin, Harry R., 1349
Rudwick, Elliott M., 780, 2114, 2115, 2125, 2126
Rugg, Harold, 1904
Rumble, Wilfrid E., Jr., 832
Ryley, Thomas W., 1232

Safford, Jeffrey J., 1144
Sage, Leland D., 205, 570
Sageser, A. Bower, 206, 353
Saloutos, Theodore, 479, 480, 481, 482, 1598, 1599, 1796, 1797
Sandmeyer, Elmer C., 1145, 2198
Sappington, Roger E., 439, 1977
Saveth, Edward A., 2199
Saxton, Alexander, 354, 1716
Schaffer, Ronald, 2240
Scheiber, Harry N., 781, 782, 1350, 2127, 2200
Scheiber, Jane, 782, 2127
Scheinberg, Stephen J., 571, 1717
Scheiner, Seth M., 572, 2128, 2129
Schieber, Clara E., 1081
Schirmer, Daniel B., 969
Schlebecker, John T., 1600
Schlesinger, Arthur M., Jr., 28, 29
Schlipp, Paul A., 1905
Schluter, William C., 1454
Schmidt, Hans, 1040
Schmitt, Bernadotte E., 1233
Schneider, Herbert W., 1869, 1978
Schneider, Robert W., 2019
Scholes, Marie V., 913, 1041
Scholes, Walter V., 913, 1041
Schultz, Stanley K., 456
Schurr, Sam H., 1491
Schwartz, Anna Jacobson, 1387
Scott, Emmet J., 2130
Scott, James B., 1042, 1082, 1083, 1146
Scott, Roy V., 1574
Scroggs, William O., 2131
Seager, Henry R., 66, 682, 1455, 1582
Sears, Louis M., 970
Seidman, Joel, 1718
Selekman, Ben M., 1719
Sellers, James B., 355

INDEX

Seltzer, Lawrence H., 1575
Semonche, John E., 207, 272
Severson, Robert F., Jr., 1531
Seymour, Charles, 208, 636, 637, 1234, 1235, 1351, 1352
Seymour, Harold, 1833
Shannon, David A., 863, 864
Shannon, Fred A., 483, 1601
Shapiro, Stanley, 783, 1720
Sharfman, I. L., 67, 683, 1456, 1576, 1577
Shepardson, Whitney H., 1602
Sherman, Richard B., 356, 573, 2132
Shipee, Lester B., 971, 972
Shover, John L., 357, 1721
Shryock, Richard H., 1934, 1935
Silk, Leonard S., 1623
Simkins, Francis B., 209, 484
Sims, William S., 1353
Sinclair, Upton, 457, 2020
Siney, Marion, 1236, 1237
Sizer, Theodore R., 1906
Slosson, Preston W., 784
Smalley, Orange A., 1532
Smith, Daniel M., 785, 1238, 1239, 1240, 1354
Smith, Darrell Hevenor, 1722
Smith, Gibbs M., 865, 1723
Smith, James W., 1979
Smith, John S., 638, 1724
Smith, Richard K., 1624
Smith, Rixey, 210, 684
Smith, T. Lynn, 2133
Smith, Timothy L., 1798, 1907
Smith, Willard H., 440, 2134
Smith, William C., 1799
Smuts, Robert W., 1834, 2241
Smythe, Donald, 211
Snell, John L., 1355, 1356
Sochen, June, 2135, 2242, 2243
Solvick, Stanley D., 574
Soule, George, 1395
Southern, David W., 273, 2136
Spaeth, Sigmund G., 2021
Spargo, John, 1357
Spear, Allan H., 2137
Spector, Ronald, 1043
Spencer, Samuel R., Jr., 2138
Spero, Sterling D., 2139
Sperry, Willard L., 1980
Spiller, Robert E., 30, 2022
Spindler, Arno, 1241
Sprague, O. M. W., 1483
Sprout, Harold, 914

Sprout, Margaret, 914
Squires, James D., 1242
Stanley, Peter W., 1147
Staples, Henry L., 358, 1578
Starr, Mark, 1658
Startt, James D., 1358, 1359, 1360
Stauffer, Alvin P., Jr., 2201
Steel, Edward M., 1725, 2244
Steelman, Joseph F., 359, 360, 575
Steelman, Lala Carr, 418, 1148, 2245
Steffens, Lincoln, 212, 361, 362, 458, 2055
Steigerwalt, Albert K., 1533, 1534
Stelzle, Charles, 441, 1981
Stephenson, George M., 213, 363, 1044, 1800
Stephenson, Nathaniel W., 214, 576
Stevens, William H. S., 1457
Stewart, Bryce M., 1726
Stewart, Frank M., 364
Stigler, George J., 1835, 2246
Stone, Ralph A., 1361, 1362
Strakhovsky, Leonid I., 1363
Strom, Sharon Hartman, 2247
Strong, Bryan, 866
Stroud, Gene S., 31
Stuart, Graham H., 915
Sturdivant, Frederick D., 1532
Suffern, Arthur E., 1727
Sullivan, Mark, 68, 215, 2056
Sutton, Walter A., 685, 1243
Swain, Donald C., 475
Swanberg, W. A., 216, 217, 973, 974, 2057, 2058
Sward, Keith T., 1579
Sweet, William W., 1982
Swisher, Carl B., 786, 787, 2202
Sydenstricker, Edgar, 1691
Sylla, Richard, 1484
Syrett, Harold C., 1244

Taft, Philip, 64, 788, 1712, 1728, 1729, 1730, 1731
Tager, Jack, 274, 365, 509
Tannenbaum, Frank, 2203
Tansill, Charles C., 1045
Tarbell, Ida M., 1535
Tarr, Joel A., 218
Tate, Merze, 1149
Taussig, Frank W., 69, 686
Taylor, A. Elizabeth, 366, 2248
Taylor, Albion Guilford, 1732
Taylor, Joseph H., 1801, 2204

Taylor, Walter F., 2023
Temperley, H. W. V., 1364
Thelen, David P., 219, 275, 276, 367, 368, 577, 639
Thomas, William I., 1802, 1836
Thomas, Woodlief, 1501
Thompson, Arthur W., 867
Thompson, Carl W., 1603
Thompson, Clarence B., 1536
Thompson, J. A., 789
Thompson, John M., 1365
Thompson, Tracy E., 1537
Thompson, Warren S., 1411
Thorburn, Neil, 790
Thorelli, Hans B., 70, 1458
Thornbrough, Emma Lou, 578, 2059, 2060, 2140, 2141
Thornthwaite, C. Warren, 1412
Thorp, Willard L., 1538, 2024
Thorson, Winston B., 1084, 1150
Thurber, Evangeline, 764
Thurston, William N., 791
Tillman, Seth P., 1366
Timberlake, James H., 277
Tindall, George B., 71, 640
Tinsley, James A., 369, 579
Tirpitz, Alfred von, 1245
Tishler, Hace S., 419
Tobey, James A., 1936
Tobin, Harold J., 792
Todd, A. L., 687, 833
Tolman, William H., 1733
Tompkins, E. Berkeley, 975
Towley, Louis, 388
Trani, Eugene P., 1151, 1367
Trask, David F., 1368
Trattner, Walter I., 793
Treat, Payson J., 1152
Trow, Clifford W., 1046
True, Alfred C., 1604
Truesdale, Leon E., 1591, 1605
Tulchin, Joseph S., 1047
Tupper, Eleanor, 1153
Turlington, Edgar W., 794, 1048
Tuttle, William H., 1734
Tuttle, William M., Jr., 795, 2142
Tweton, D. Jerome, 1606
Twiss, Benjamin R., 834
Tyack, David B., 1908
Tyler, Robert L., 868, 1735, 1736

Unterberger, Betty M., 1369, 1370
Urofsky, Melvin I., 220, 278, 508, 641, 688, 689, 1459, 1539

Vagts, Alfred, 1085, 1086
Van Alstyne, Richard W., 1246, 1247
Vance, Maurice M., 221, 510
Van Kleeck, Mary, 1719
Van Riper, Paul P., 580
Van Tassel, David D., 1909
Van Tine, Warren R., 1737
Varg, Paul A., 1154, 1155, 1156, 1157, 1158
Vecoli, Rudolph J., 1803
Vevier, Charles, 1159, 1160
Veysey, Laurence R., 642, 1910
Viereck, George Sylvester, 796, 1248
Villard, Oswald Garrison, 222, 2061

Wade, Louise C., 223, 420
Wakstein, Allen M., 1738
Wald, Lillian D., 224, 421, 2249
Walker, Forrest A., 422
Wall, Louise H., 160, 620
Walworth, Arthur, 225, 643, 1249, 1371
Warburg, Paul M., 690, 691, 1485
Ward, Alan J., 1087
Ward, Robert D., 797
Warner, Hoyt Landon, 370
Warner, Robert M., 581
Warren, Charles, 835
Warshow, Herman T., 1540
Warth, Robert D., 798, 2205
Washington, Booker T., 226, 2143
Watkins, Gordon S., 799, 1739
Watkins, Myron W., 72, 1460
Watson, Richard L., Jr., 32
Watterson, Henry, 227, 2062
Way, Royal B., 972
Weaver, Norman F., 2206
Wefald, Jon, 1804
Weinberg, Albert K., 976
Weinberg, Sydney, 800
Weinstein, Edwin A., 644, 645, 801, 802
Weinstein, James, 371, 803, 869, 870, 1250, 1396
Weintraub, Hyman, 1740
Weiss, Nancy J., 228, 372, 692, 2144, 2145
Welch, Richard E., Jr., 977, 978, 1983
Welles, Sumner, 1049
Wells, Samuel F., Jr., 916
Werking, Richard H., 917
Wesley, Charles H., 2146

INDEX

Wesser, Robert F., 373, 423
West, George P., 1741
Weston, Rubin F., 979
Whelpton, P. K., 1411, 1742
White, John A., 1161, 1162
White, Morton, 511, 1871
White, Ronald C., Jr., 442
White, Walter, 2147
White, William Allen, 229, 2063
Whiteman, Harold B., Jr., 1372
Whitener, Daniel J., 374
Whittaker, William G., 980
Wiebe, Robert H., 73, 279, 582, 583
Wilcox, Clair, 1461
Wilcox, Delos F., 1580, 1581
Wild, John, 1870
Wilensky, Norman M., 584
Wilkerson, Marcus M., 981
Willard, George-Anne, 2148
Willcox, Walter F., 1413, 1805
Williams, Benjamin H., 918
Williams, Michael, 804, 1984
Williams, William A., 919, 982, 983
Williamson, Harold F., 1397
Willis, Henry Parker, 693, 1486
Willoughby, William F., 805
Wilson, Harold S., 459, 2064
Wilson, Louis R., 1911
Wilson, Robert Frost, 723
Wimer, Kurt, 1373, 1374, 1375
Winter, Ella, 230, 460, 2065
Wisan, Joseph E., 984
Wisbey, Herbert A., Jr., 1985
Wiseman, John B., 585, 2149
Wish, Harvey, 2150
Witte, Edwin E., 1743
Wittke, Carl, 806, 1806, 1807, 1808,
    2066, 2207, 2208

Wolcott, Leon O., 1590
Wolgemuth, Kathleen L., 694, 2151
Wolman, Leo, 1744, 1745
Wood, James P., 2067
Wood, Norman J., 1541
Wood, Stephen B., 424, 836
Woodbury, Robert M., 1746
Woods, Robert A., 425
Woodson, Carter G., 2089
Woodward, C. Vann, 231, 375, 485,
    2152, 2153
Woofter, Thomas J., 1809, 2154
Woolbert, Robert Gale, 33
Woytanowitz, George M., 1912
Wreszin, Michael, 232, 807
Wright, Frank Lloyd, 2025, 2026
Wright, Herbert F., 1050, 1088, 1163
Wright, Philip G., 1492
Wynes, Charles E., 2155

Yates, Louis A. R., 1376
Yearley, Clifton K., 74
Yellen, Samuel, 1747
Yellowitz, Irwin, 376, 1748
Yeomans, Henry A., 1913
Young, George Berkeley, 893
Young, James H., 1937

Zabriskie, Edward H., 1164
Zacharewicz, Mary Misela, 1377
Zaturenska, Marya, 2003
Zeis, Paul M., 1582
Zimmerman, Jane, 426
Zink, Harold, 377
Zivojinovic, Dragan R., 1378, 1379
Zmaniecki, Florian, 1802, 1836
Zucker, Norman L., 233, 378

NOTES